John R. Sweney

Bright Melodies for the Sunday School and Young People's Societies

John R. Sweney

Bright Melodies for the Sunday School and Young People's Societies

ISBN/EAN: 9783337155506

Printed in Europe, USA, Canada, Australia, Japan

Cover: Foto ©Thomas Meinert / pixelio.de

More available books at **www.hansebooks.com**

Bright Melodies

FOR

THE SUNDAY SCHOOL AND YOUNG PEOPLE'S SOCIETIES

Embracing Praise Hymns, Work Songs,
Invitation Songs, Primary Songs,
etc., etc.

EDITORS:

JNO. R. SWENEY and J. HOWARD ENTWISLE

PUBLISHED BY

JOHN J. HOOD

PHILADELPHIA
1024 Arch St.

CHICAGO
940 W. Madison St.

Copyright 1899, by John J. Hood.

Price, 30 cts. $25 per Hundred.

THE TEN COMMANDMENTS.

1. Thou shalt have no other gods before me.

2. Thou shalt not make unto thee any graven image, or any likeness of *any thing* that *is* in heaven above, or that *is* in the earth beneath, or that *is* in the water under the earth: thou shalt not bow down thyself to them, nor serve them: for I the Lord thy God *am* a jealous God, visiting the iniquity of the fathers upon the children unto the third and fourth *generation* of them that hate me; and showing mercy unto thousands of them that love me, and keep my commandments.

3. Thou shalt not take the name of the Lord thy God in vain: for the Lord will not hold him guiltless that taketh his name in vain.

4. Remember the Sabbath day, to keep it holy. Six days shalt thou labor, and do all thy work: but the seventh day *is* the Sabbath of the Lord thy God: *in it* thou shalt not do any work, thou, nor **thy** son, nor thy daughter, thy manservant, nor thy maidservant, nor thy cattle, nor thy stranger that *is* within thy gates: for *in* six days the Lord made heaven and earth, the sea, and all that in them *is*, and rested the seventh day: wherefore the Lord blessed the Sabbath day, and hallowed it.

5. Honor thy father and thy mother: that thy days may be long upon the land which the Lord thy God giveth thee.

6. Thou shalt not kill.

7. Thou shalt not commit adultery.

8. Thou shalt not steal.

9. Thou shalt not bear false witness against thy neighbor.

10. Thou shalt not covet thy neighbor's house, thou shalt not covet thy neighbor's wife, nor his manservant, nor his maidservant, nor his ox, nor his ass, nor anything that *is* thy neighbor's.—Ex. 20: 3–17.

SUMMARY OF THE COMMANDMENTS.

Jesus said unto him, Thou shalt love the Lord thy God with all thy heart, and with all thy soul, and with all thy mind. This is the first and great commandment. And the second *is* like unto it, Thou shalt love thy neighbor as thyself. On these two commandments hang all the law and the prophets.—Matt. 22: 37–40.

Suffer Little Children to come unto me and forbid them not: for of such is the Kingdom of God.

THE LORD'S PRAYER.

Our Father which art in heaven, hallowed be thy name. Thy kingdom come. Thy will be done in earth, as *it is* in heaven. Give us this day our daily bread. And forgive us our debts, as we forgive our debtors. And lead us not into temptation, but deliver us from evil: For thine is the kingdom, and the power, and the glory, for ever. Amen.—Matt. 6: 9-13.

THE APOSTLES' CREED.

I believe in God the Father Almighty, Maker of heaven and earth. And in Jesus Christ his only begotten Son our Lord: who was conceived by the Holy Ghost, born of the Virgin Mary; suffered under Pontius Pilate, was crucified, dead and buried; he descended into hades;* the third day he rose from the dead; he ascended into heaven; and sitteth at the right hand of God the Father Almighty; from thence he shall come to judge the quick and the dead. I believe in the Holy Ghost; the holy catholic † Church, the communion of saints, the forgiveness of sins; the resurrection of the body, and the life everlasting. Amen.

BEATITUDES.

Blessed *are* the poor in spirit: for theirs is the kingdom of heaven.

Blessed *are* they that mourn: for they shall be comforted.

Blessed *are* the meek: for they shall inherit the earth.

Blessed *are* they which do hunger and thirst after righteousness: for they shall be filled.

Blessed *are* the merciful: for they shall obtain mercy.

Blessed *are* the pure in heart: for they shall see God.

Blessed *are* the peacemakers: for they shall be called the children of God.

Blessed *are* they which are persecuted for righteousness' sake: for theirs is the kingdom of heaven.

Blessed are ye, when *men* shall revile you, and persecute *you*, and shall say all manner of evil against you falsely, for my sake.

*The place of departed spirits.   † The whole Christian.

Little Children, love one another.

BRIGHT MELODIES.

Gloria Patri.

Charles Meineke.

Glo-ry be to the Father, and to the Son, and to the Ho-ly Ghost, as it was in the be-gin-ning, is now, and ev-er shall be, world without end. A-men, a-men.

Doxology.

Tune, OLD HUNDRED. L. M.

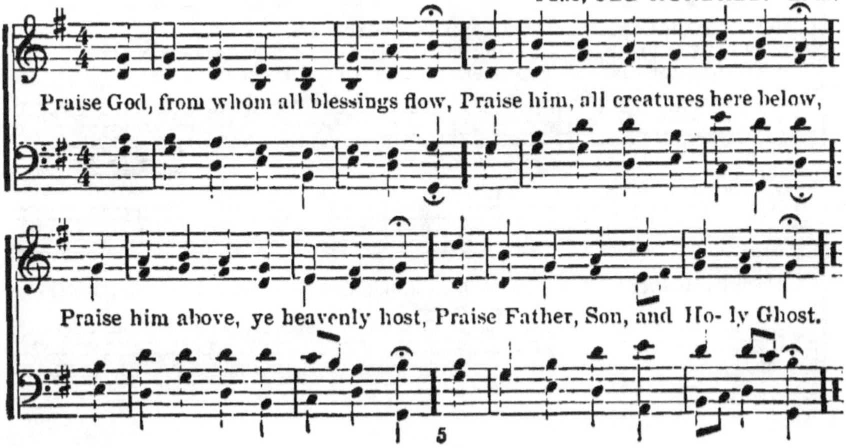

Praise God, from whom all blessings flow, Praise him, all creatures here below, Praise him above, ye heavenly host, Praise Father, Son, and Ho-ly Ghost.

On to Victory.—CONCLUDED.

Onward in the conflict, hop-ing, trusting, On to vic-to-ry!

Be of Good Cheer.

CHARLOTTE ABBEY. "Be of good cheer: It is I; be not afraid."—Mark vi: 60. FRANK M. DAVIS.

1. "Be of good cheer," saith the Saviour, "Tho' all thy brightest hopes fade;
2. "Be of good cheer, tho' the tempter And world are 'gainst thee array'd;
3. "Be of good cheer thro' thy tri-als; On me let burdens be laid;

I will be near to sus-tain thee; It is I, O be not a-fraid."
I will give grace that will conquer; It is I, O be not a-fraid."
Tho' they be heavy, I'll bear them; It is I, O be not a-fraid."

CHORUS.
It is I, ... it is I, ... It is I, O be not a-fraid!
It is I, it is I,

"Be of good cheer," saith the Saviour; "It is I, O be not a-fraid!"

From "Notes of Praise." By per. of John J. Hood.

Jesus Leads.

"And when he putteth forth his own sheep, he goeth before them, and the sheep follow him; for they know his voice."—John x: 4.

JOHN R. CLEMENTS. JNO. R. SWENEY.

Andante.

1. Like a shepherd, tender, true, Je-sus leads, . . . Je-sus leads, . .
2. All a-long life's rugged road Je-sus leads, . . . Je-sus leads, . .
3. Thro' the sun-lit ways of life Je-sus leads, . . . Je-sus leads, . .

Dai-ly finds us pastures new, Je-sus leads, . . . Je-sus leads; . .
Till we reach yon blest a-bode, Je-sus leads, . . . Je-sus leads; . .
Thro' the war-ings and the strife Je-sus leads, . . . Je-sus leads; . .

If thick mists are o'er the way, . . Or the flock 'mid danger feeds, . .
All the way, . before, he's trod, . And he now . . the flock precedes, . .
When we reach . the Jordan's tide, Where life's bound-'ry-line re-cedes, . .

He will watch them lest they stray, Je-sus leads, . . Je-sus leads.
Safe in-to the fold of God Je-sus leads, . . Je-sus leads.
He will spread the waves a-side, Je-sus leads, . . Je-sus leads.

Copyright, 1895, by Jno. R. Sweney.

The Glad Home-Gathering

ADA BLENKHORN.   J. HOWARD ENTWISLE.

1. By and by I know there'll be, by the shining crystal sea, Such a
2. Friend with friend again will meet, O the welcome will be sweet, At the
3. Christ the Lamb shall be our light, we shall walk with him in white, At the
4. There's an in-vi-ta-tion free, and it comes to you and me, To the
5. Praise the Lord! I'm go-ing too, now by faith the scene I view, At the

glad home-gath'ring by and by; When we walk the golden strand in that
glad home-gath'ring by and by; We shall meet to part no more on that
glad home-gath'ring by and by; He will wipe a-way our tears, he will
glad home-gath'ring by and by; Who-so-ev-er will may share in the
glad home-gath'ring by and by; By his grace and mer-cy free, with the

CHORUS.

bright and blessed land, At the glad home-gath'ring by and by. There will be a
fair and blissful shore, At the glad home-gath'ring by and by.
banish all our fears, At the glad home-gath'ring by and by.
joyful meeting there, At the glad home-gath'ring by and by.
ransomed I will be, At the glad home-gath'ring by and by.

glad home-gath'ring by and by, There will be a glad home-gath'ring by and by; When [the

Lord shall bid us come to his bright, celestial home, To the glad home-gath'ring by [and by.

Copyright, 1899, by J. Howard Entwisle.

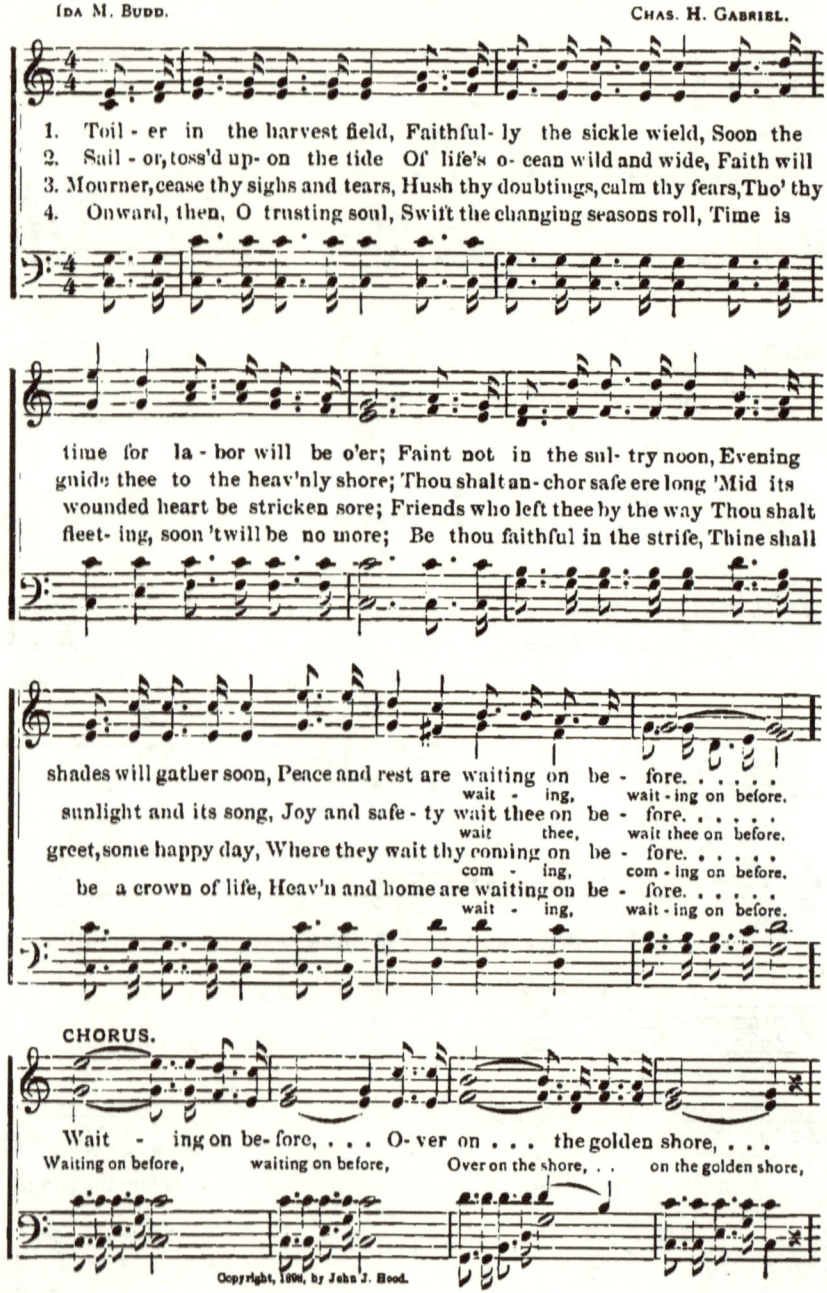

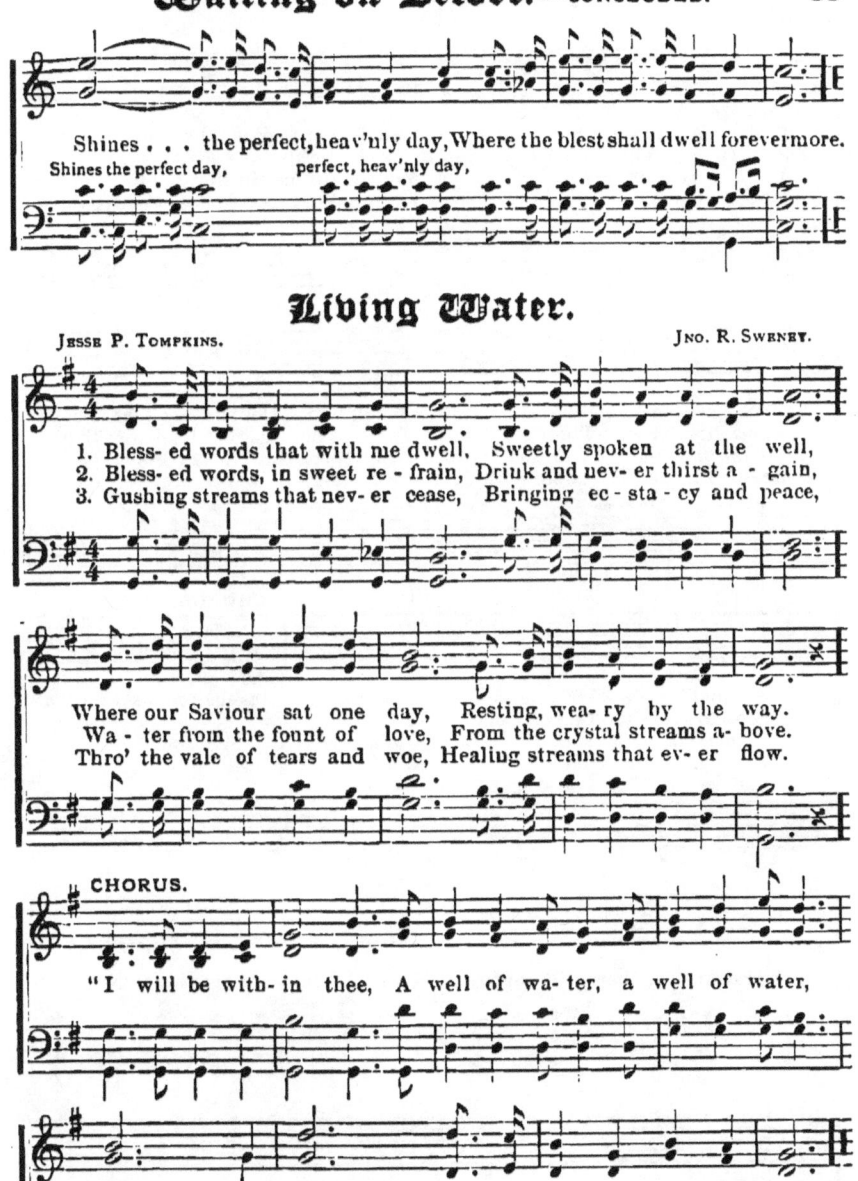

14. Jesus Promised Me a Home.

H. LUTTON.   JNO. R. SWENEY.

1. There's a place in heav'n pre-pared for me, When the toils of this life are o'er; Where the saints, rob'd in white, shall for-ev-er be, Singing prais-es for-ev-er-more.
2. In my Fa-ther's home are mansions bright, Je-sus says it and I know 'tis true; There's a home for me, in that land of light, Brother, sis-ter, there is one for you.
3. Ma-ny dear ones we lov'd are be-fore the throne, In that happy, happy home on high; I shall walk with them thro' the streets of gold, I shall wear a star-ry crown by and by.
4. In that home a-bove, be-yond the skies, Soon from sickness, pain and death I'll be, There with Je-sus to reign for-ev-er-more, Through-out all e-ter-ni-ty.

CHORUS.

Je-sus promis'd me a home o-ver there, Je-sus promis'd me a home o-ver there; No more sickness, sorrow, pain or death, Je-sus promis'd me a home o-ver there.

Copyright, 1880, by Jno. R. Sweney.

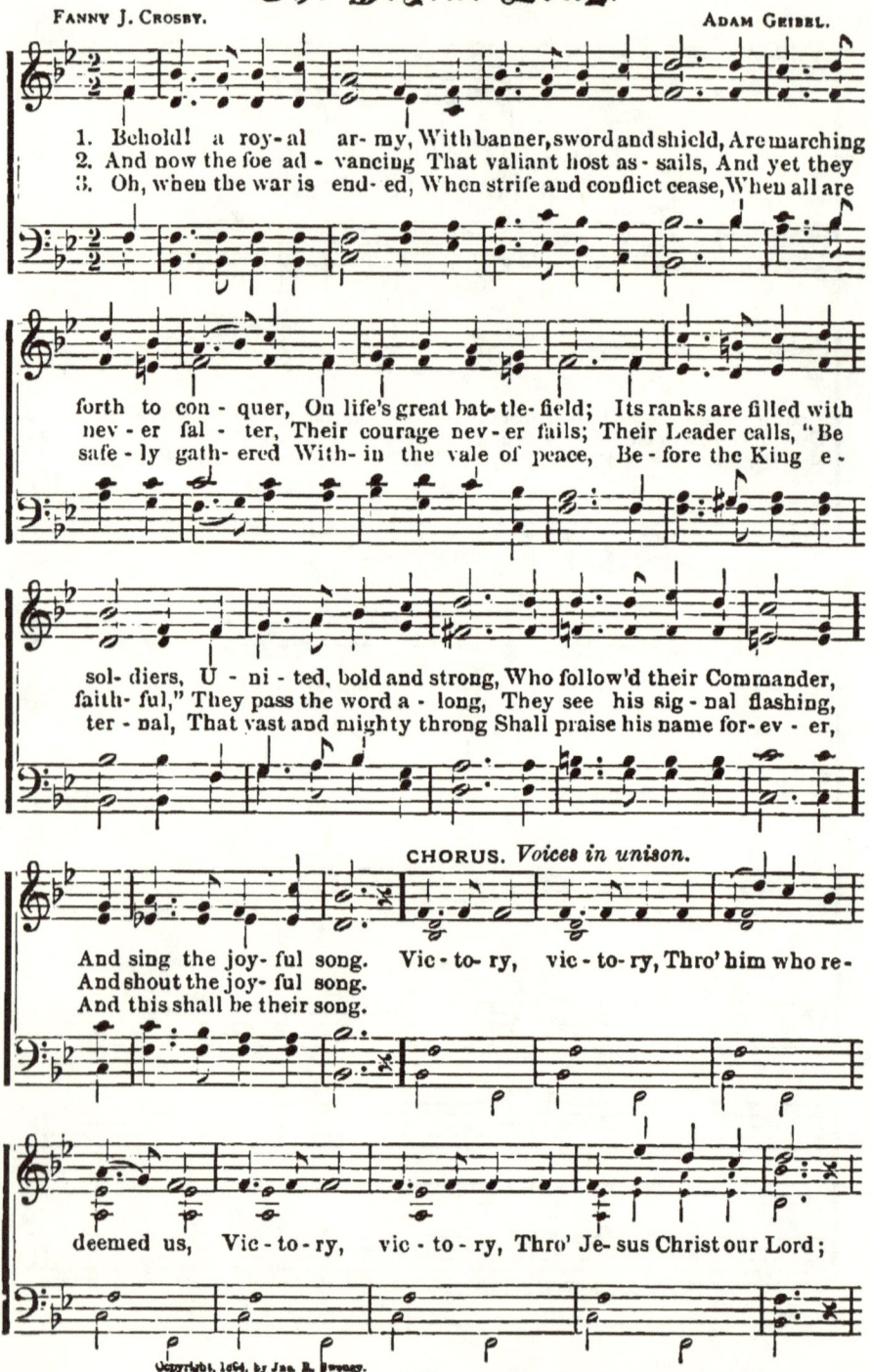

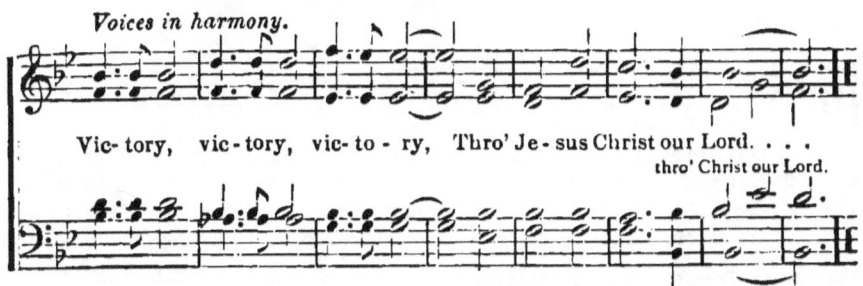
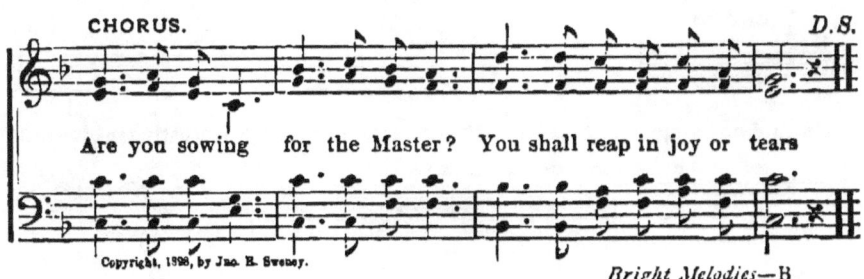

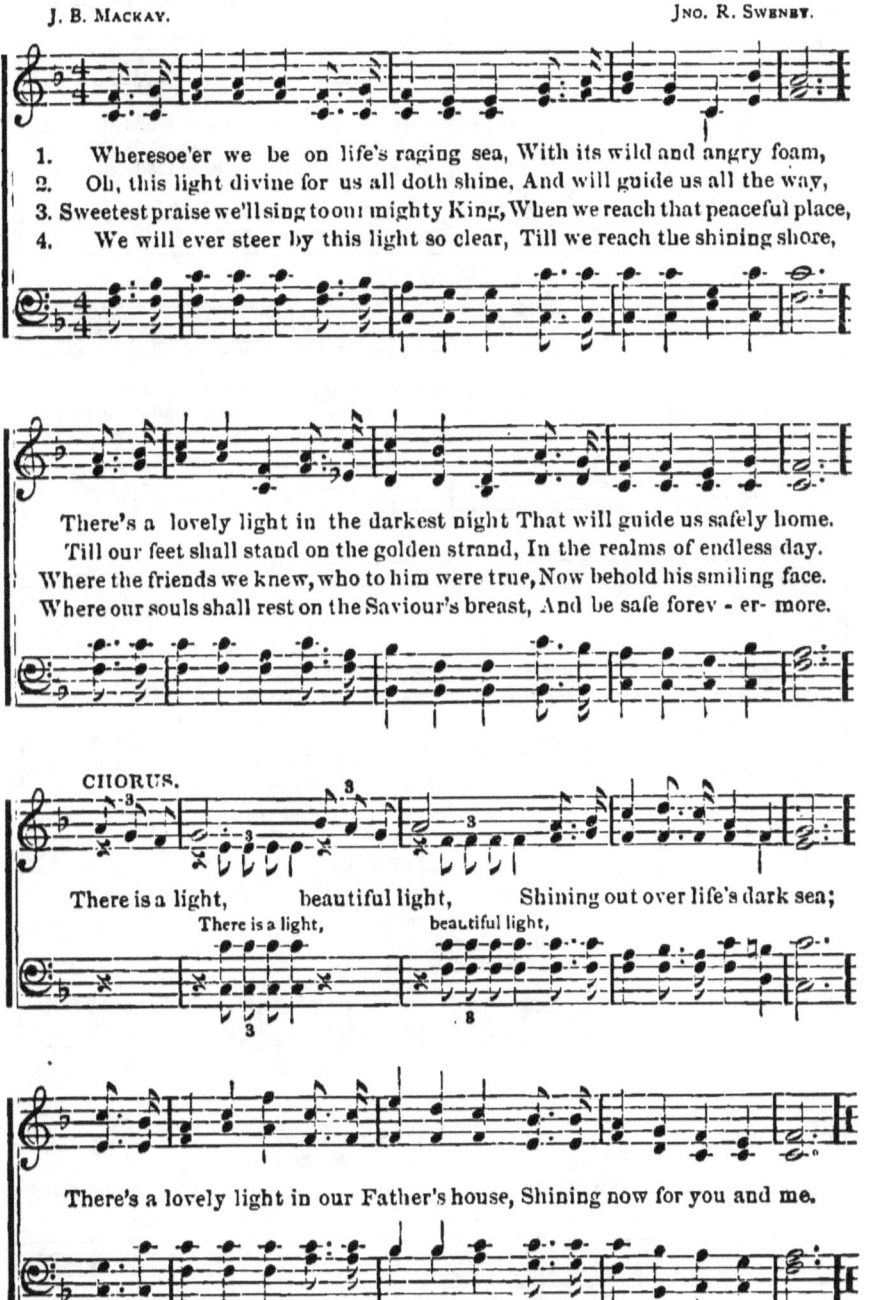

Will You Be One?—CONCLUDED.

Ev-er rejoic-ing at Jesus' right hand, Will you be one? . . .
Will you be one by and by?

Wait On the Lord.

FANNY J. CROSBY. JNO. R. SWENEY.

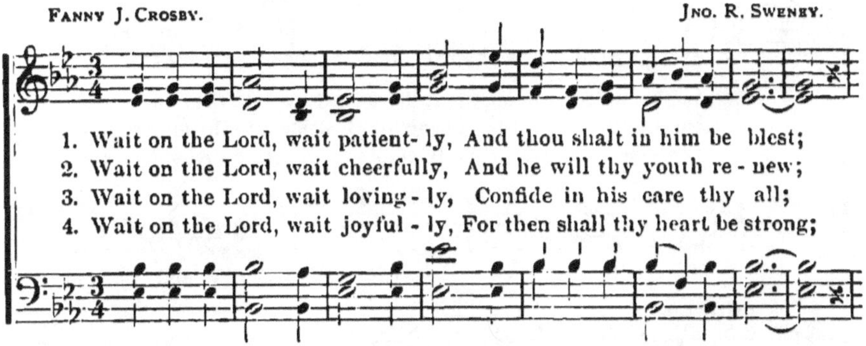

1. Wait on the Lord, wait patient-ly, And thou shalt in him be blest;
2. Wait on the Lord, wait cheerfully, And he will thy youth re-new;
3. Wait on the Lord, wait loving-ly, Confide in his care thy all;
4. Wait on the Lord, wait joyful-ly, For then shall thy heart be strong;

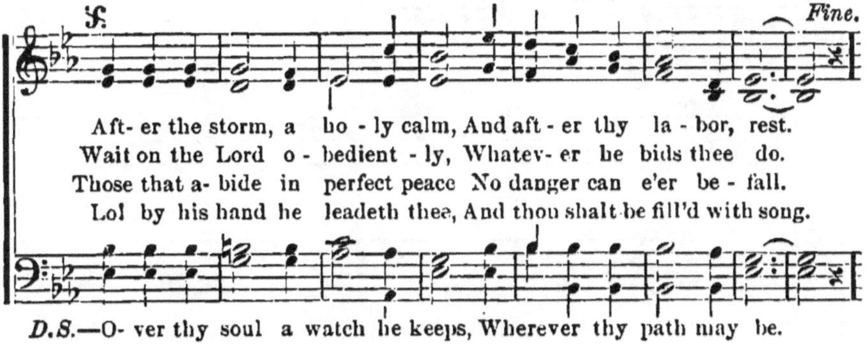

Fine.

Aft-er the storm, a ho-ly calm, And aft-er thy la-bor, rest.
Wait on the Lord o-bedient-ly, Whatev-er he bids thee do.
Those that a-bide in perfect peace No danger can e'er be-fall.
Lo! by his hand he leadeth thee, And thou shalt be fill'd with song.

D.S.—O-ver thy soul a watch he keeps, Wherever thy path may be.

CHORUS. *D.S.*

Wait on the Lord, for whom hast thou On earth or in heaven but he? . . .
but he?

Copyright, 1892, by Jno. R. Sweney.

Upon the Rock.

IDA M. BUDD.
CHAS H. GABRIEL.

1. Up-on the Rock, the solid Rock I'm building, day by day, A house no storms can overthrow, no floods can wash a-way; For Christ its sure foundation is, its precious corner stone, On him, thro' him, for him I build, the work is his alone.

2. I la-bor on se-cure in this, my Rock can never fail, Sin's waves may seek to undermine, and winds of doubt as-sail; But winds may blow, and rains descend, and storms be fierce and wild, They cannot shake my building firm on this foundation piled.

3. And oh! my heart is glad to know that he my work doth see; I have his promise that my toil not all in vain shall be, For, finished by his loving hand, my house at last shall rise, A glorious place prepared for me,—my mansion in the skies.

CHORUS. *Faster.*

Upon the Rock, ... the solid Rock .....
Against the storm, ... or tempest's shock, ...
{ Upon the Rock,
Against the storm, the solid Rock
or tempest's shock,

1.
I am building safe and sure; .....
My house shall stand (*Omit*. ....) se - cure. ......
I am building safe and sure, I am building safe and sure :
My house shall stand secure, (*Omit*. ....) My house shall stand secure.

Copyright, 1899, by John J. Hood

32. I Glory In the Cross of Christ.

IDA SCOTT TAYLOR. J. HOWARD ENTWISLE.

1. My heart to-day with joy is singing, I glo-ry in the cross of Christ;
My faith to Je-sus' love is clinging, I glo-ry in the cross of Christ.

2. His faith divine is my salvation, I glo-ry in the cross of Christ;
I'm builded on his sure foundation, I glo-ry in the cross of Christ.

3. His mer-cy all my soul is thrilling, I glo-ry in the cross of Christ;
His presence ev-'ry fear is stilling, I glo-ry in the cross of Christ.

CHORUS.

The cross, the wondrous cross, where Je-sus died for me, The cross whereon he bore my sins and made me free; I glo-ry in the cross, for there his love I see, I glo-ry in the cross of Christ.

Copyright, 1899, by J. Howard Entwisle.

4 He died for me on Calv'ry's mountain,
I glory in the cross of Christ;
He washed me in the cleansing fount-
I glory in the cross of Christ. [ain.

5 O fount of love within me swelling,
I glory in the cross of Christ;
O blessed peace my soul indwelling,
I glory in the cross of Christ.

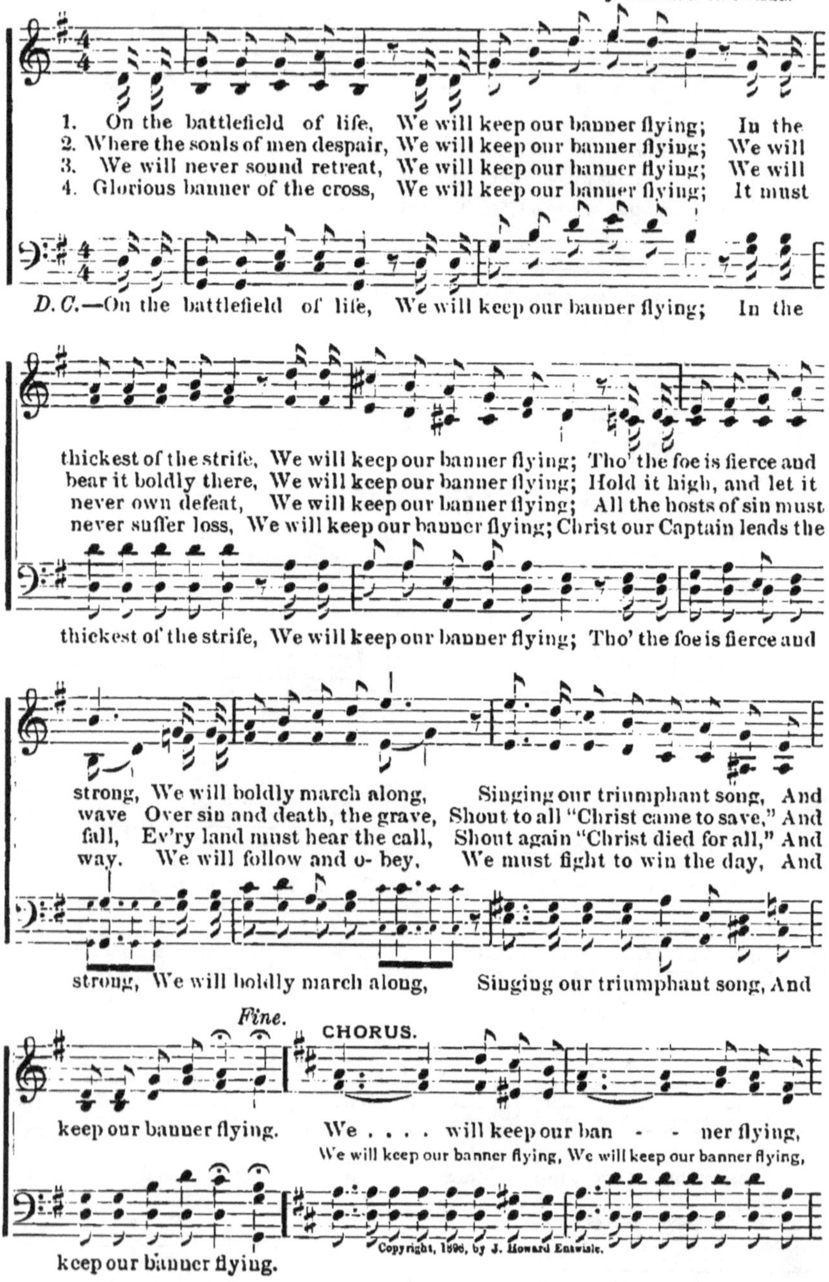

Glorious Victory.

Fanny J. Crosby.   Jno. R. Sweney.

1. Vic-tory, vic-tory, glorious vic-tory, Onward, soldiers of the Lord;
2. Vic-tory, vic-tory, glorious vic-tory, Faint not, fear not, boldly stand;
3. Vic-tory, vic-tory, glorious vic-tory Still is sounding from the sky,
4. Vic-tory, vic-tory, glorious vic-tory, Soon we'll lay our armor down;

Hear the soul-in-spiring promise, We shall conquer thro' his word.
Wave our ban-ner, shout ho-san-na, With the Spirit's sword in hand.
While be-fore our great Commander Sa-tan's vanquish'd armies fly.
Soon give up the cross for-ev-er, And re-ceive the victor's crown.

CHORUS.

We shall o-vercome the world, hal-le-lu-jah to his name,
We shall o-ver-come by faith; We shall o-vercome the world,
hal-le-lu-jah to his name, Who has triumphed o-ver death.

Copyright, 1890, by Jno. R. Sweney.

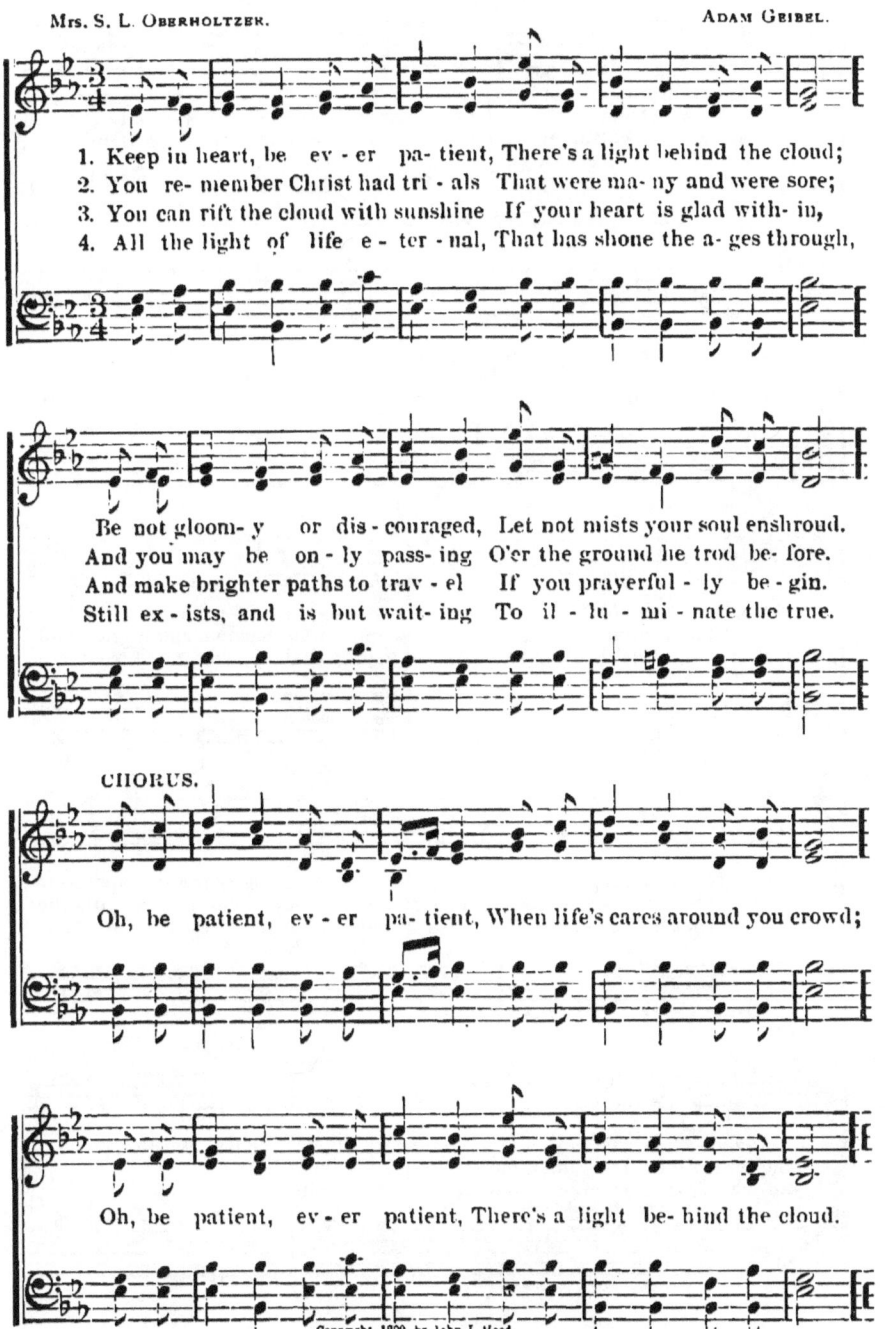

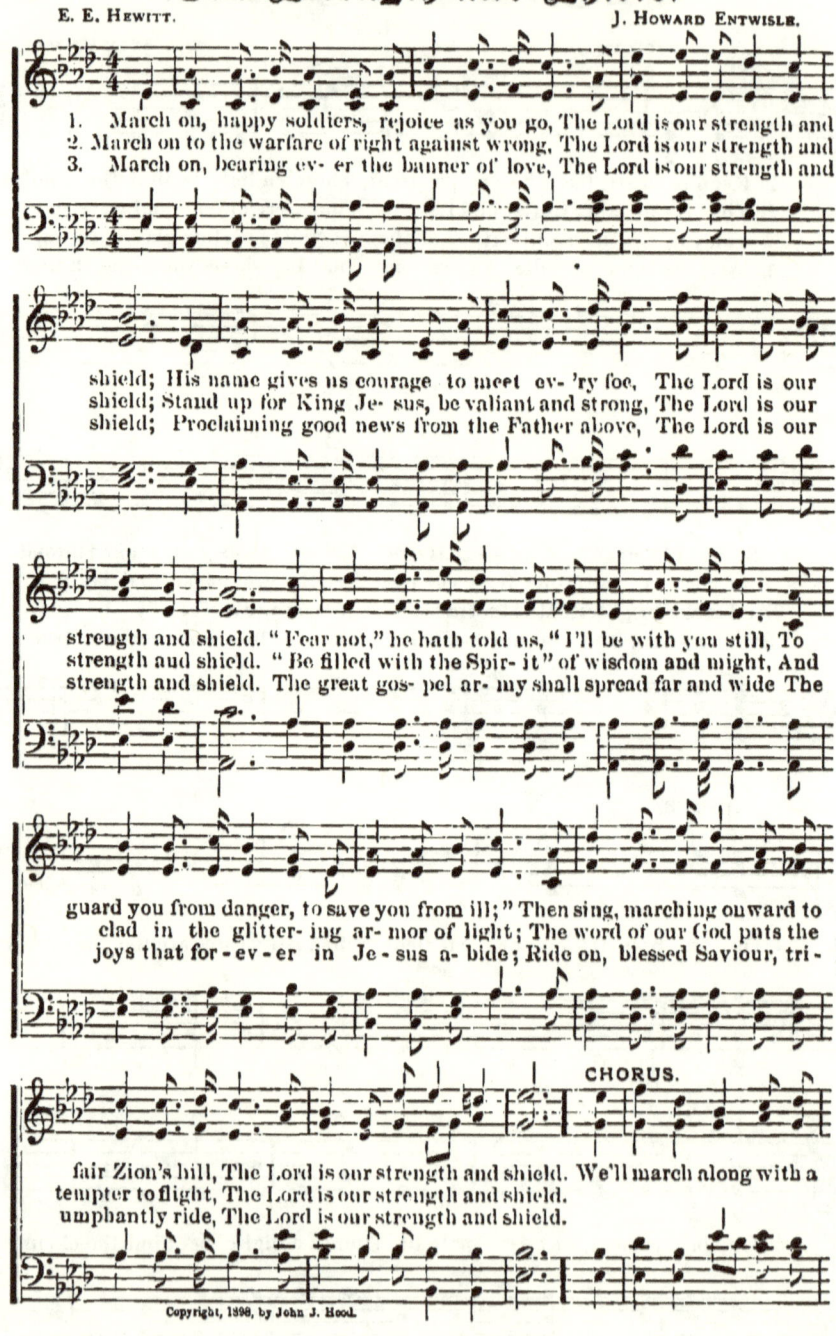

42. With Jesus.

Rev. D. W. Gordon.   Jno. R. Sweney.

1. When from the scenes of earth we rise, To find our home beyond the skies,
2. The storms of life will all be o'er, Our souls be tempest-toss'd no more,
3. Redeemed from sin and saved by grace, We shall behold his blessed face,
4. With him in glo-ry e'er to stay, Where founts of living waters play,

What visions then shall greet our eyes, When we shall be with Je-sus!
When we have reach'd the golden shore, For we shall be with Je-sus.
The wonders of his love to trace, As we shall be with Je-sus.
And sorrow's tears are wiped a-way, For-ev-er-more with Je-sus.

CHORUS.

To be with Je-sus, O how sweet! With saints and angels at his feet, With songs we shall each other greet, And ev-er be with Je-sus.

Copyright, 1879, by Jno. R. Sweney.

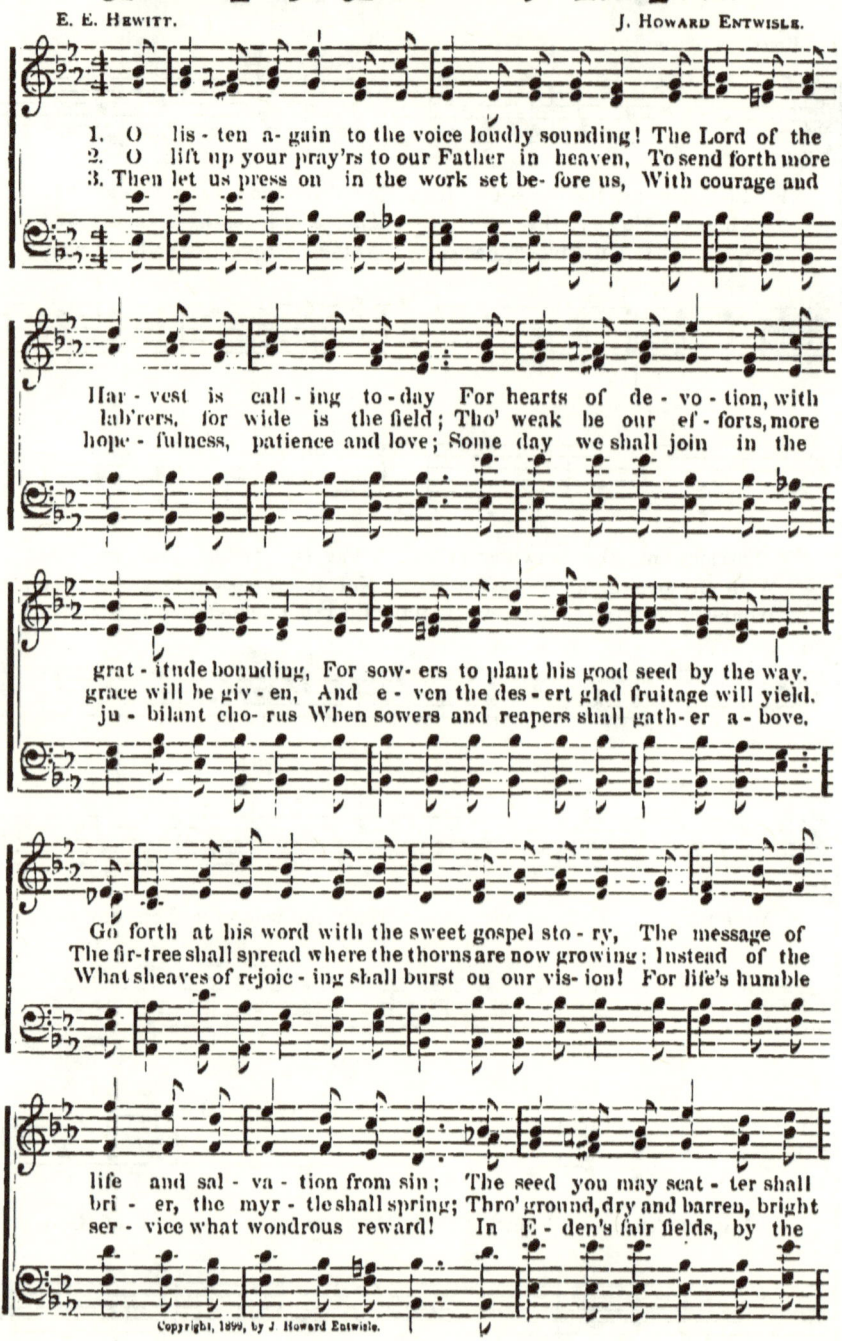

Sowing the Seed, etc.—CONCLUDED. 45

rise up in glo-ry, And sheaves, rich and golden, the toil-er shall win.
streams shall be flowing, The souls now in sor-row for gladness shall sing.
gar-ners' e-lysian, The servant shall share in the joy of the Lord.

CHORUS.

Be sow-ing, still sow-ing, The seed of the kingdom that never shall die;
Be sowing, be sowing, still sowing, still sowing,

Be sow-ing, still sow-ing, A wonderful harvest we'll reap, by and by.
Be sowing, be sowing, still sowing, still sowing,

No Tears in Yonder Home.

J. H. ENTWISLE.   For Male Voices.*   ISAAC BAKER WOODBURY.

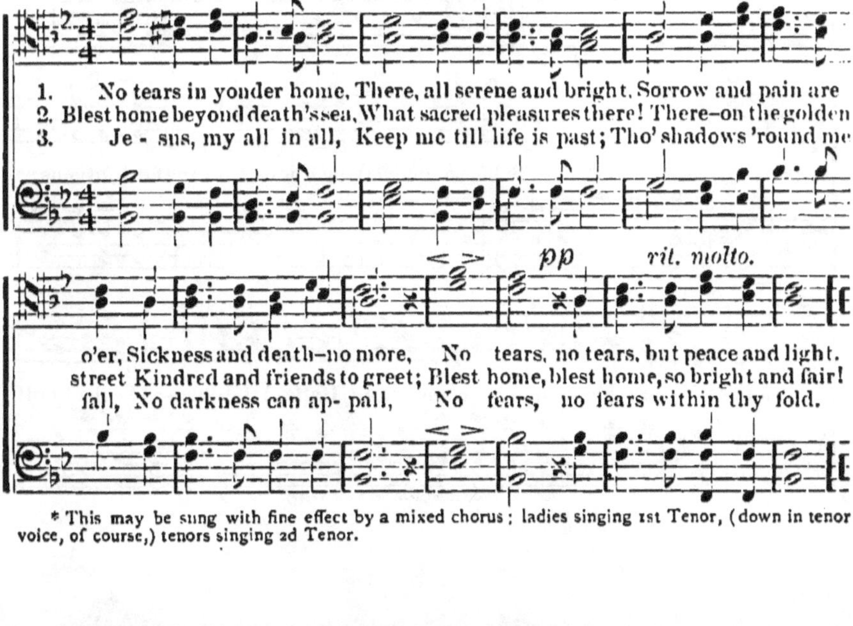

1. No tears in yonder home, There, all serene and bright, Sorrow and pain are
2. Blest home beyond death's sea, What sacred pleasures there! There—on the golden
3. Je-sus, my all in all, Keep me till life is past; Tho' shadows 'round me

pp   *rit. molto.*

o'er, Sickness and death—no more, No tears, no tears, but peace and light.
street Kindred and friends to greet; Blest home, blest home, so bright and fair!
fall, No darkness can ap-pall, No fears, no fears within thy fold.

* This may be sung with fine effect by a mixed chorus; ladies singing 1st Tenor, (down in tenor voice, of course,) tenors singing 2d Tenor.

We Come Again.—CONCLUDED.

Shout the story, glo-ry, glo-ry, Halle-lujah evermore to God our King!

Once More We Gather.

FANNY J. CROSBY. "Enter his courts with praise."—Ps. c: 4. FRANK M. DAVIS.

1. Once more we gather in our Sabbath dwelling, Singing the praises of our King;
2. Once more we gather for a joyful service, To him who's kept us all our days;
3. Once more we gather on this blessed Sabbath, Lifting our hearts in pray'r and [praise;

For all his blessings and his loving kindness, Grateful hearts to him we bring.
We will adore and laud his name forever, For his wondrous works and ways.
Jesus, to thee be all the praise and glo-ry That our youthful voices raise.

CHORUS.

Praise him, praise him, Praise the mighty King of glo-ry;
Praise him, praise him, praise him, praise him,

Praise him, praise him, Praise the mighty King of glo-ry.
Praise him, praise him, praise him, praise him,

From "Notes of Praise." By per. of John J. Hood.

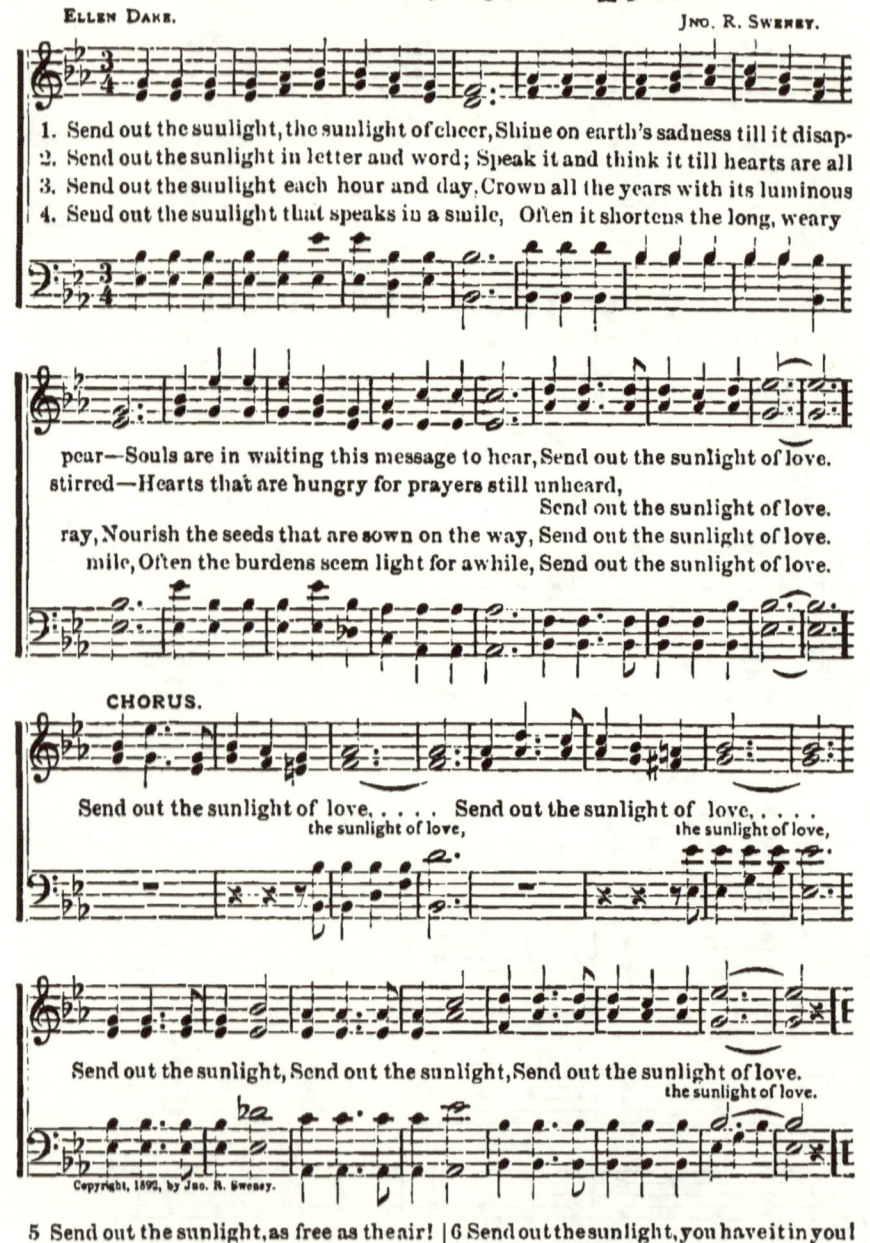

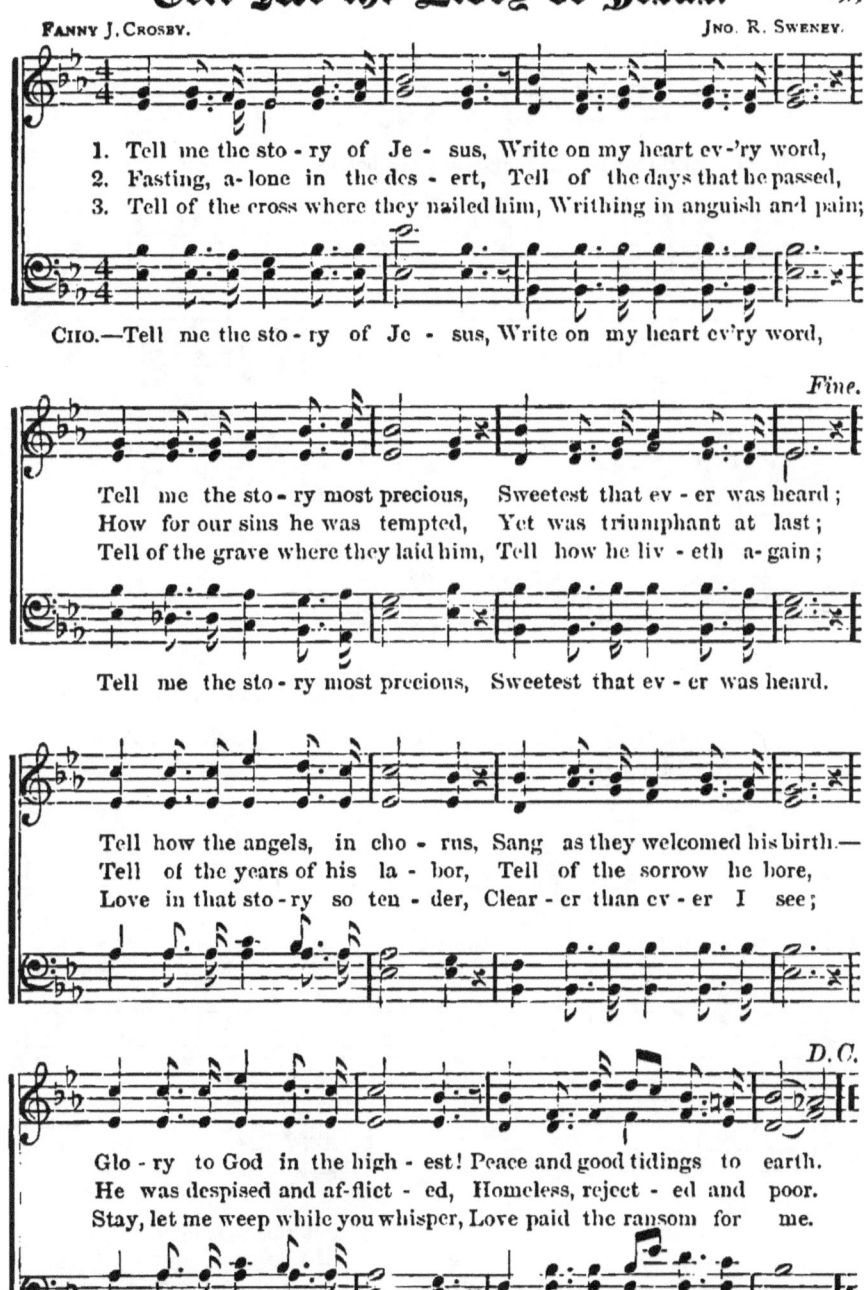

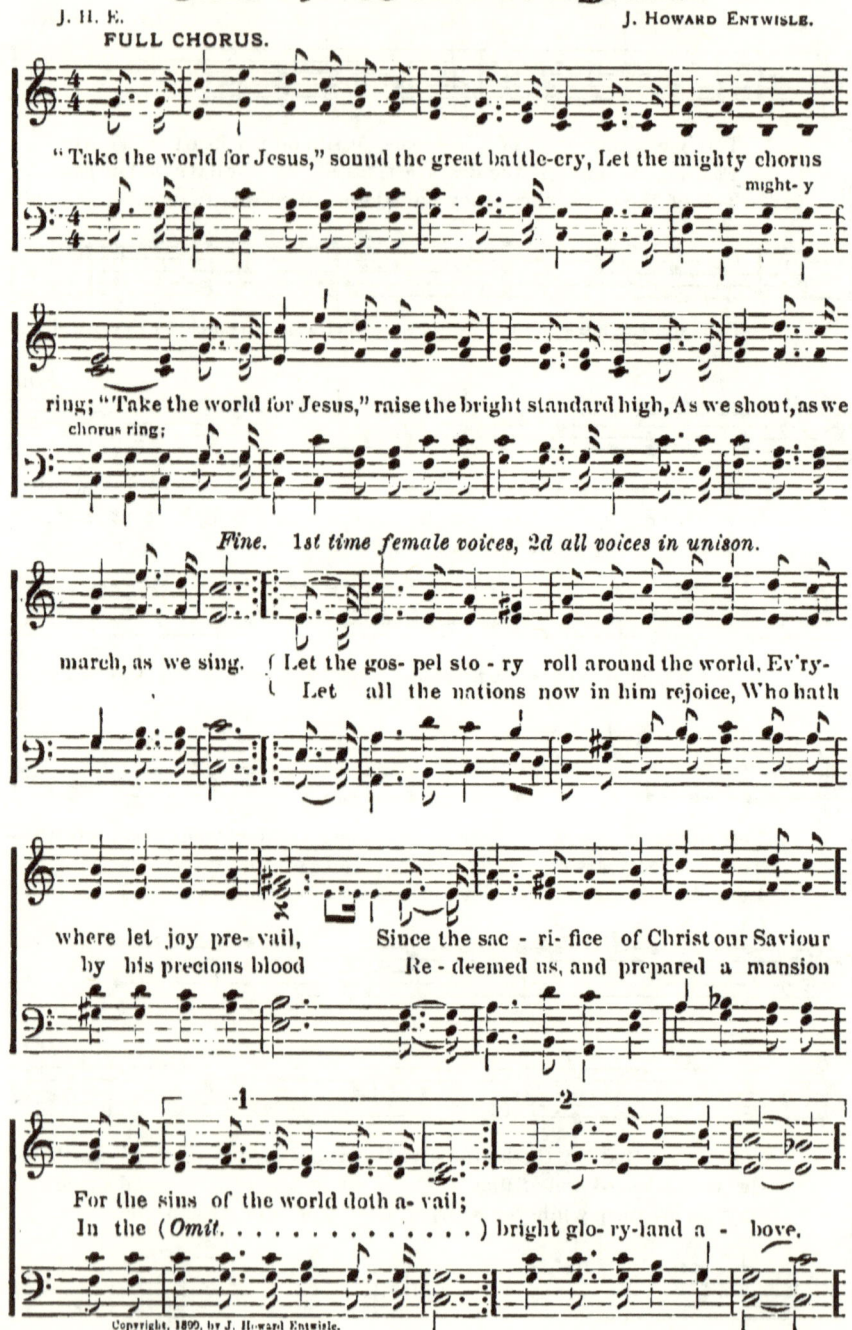

Take the World, etc.—CONCLUDED.

SEMI-CHORUS. *Smoothly.*

{ Out on the mountains of sin and despair, Millions are perishing, needing our care;
{ Tell them of Jesus who rose from the grave, Tell them of Jesus, the Mighty to Save;

D. C.

{ Shall we not send them the message to-day? Shall we not help without further delay? }
{ Plenteous salvation in him doth abound, Cleansing and healing in Jesus are found. }

He Leadeth Me.

C. H. W. Mrs. C. H. WOOLSTON.

1. He leadeth me! O words di- vine, What comfort thrills this heart of mine;
2. He leadeth me! my Shepherd, Guide, Secure- ly thro' the pastures wide;
3. He leadeth me! in sorrows he My Keeper is, where'er I be;
4. He leadeth me! his goodness tell, His mercy with his child doth dwell;

rit.

O blessed light in darkness shine,   He leadeth me! he leadeth me!
A- biding close- ly by my side,   He leadeth me! yea, leadeth me!
In shady nook or stormy sea,   He leadeth me! yea, e - ven me!
Oh, let the theme his praises swell, He leadeth me! he leadeth me!

Copyright, 1898, by Mrs. C. H. Woolston. Used by per.

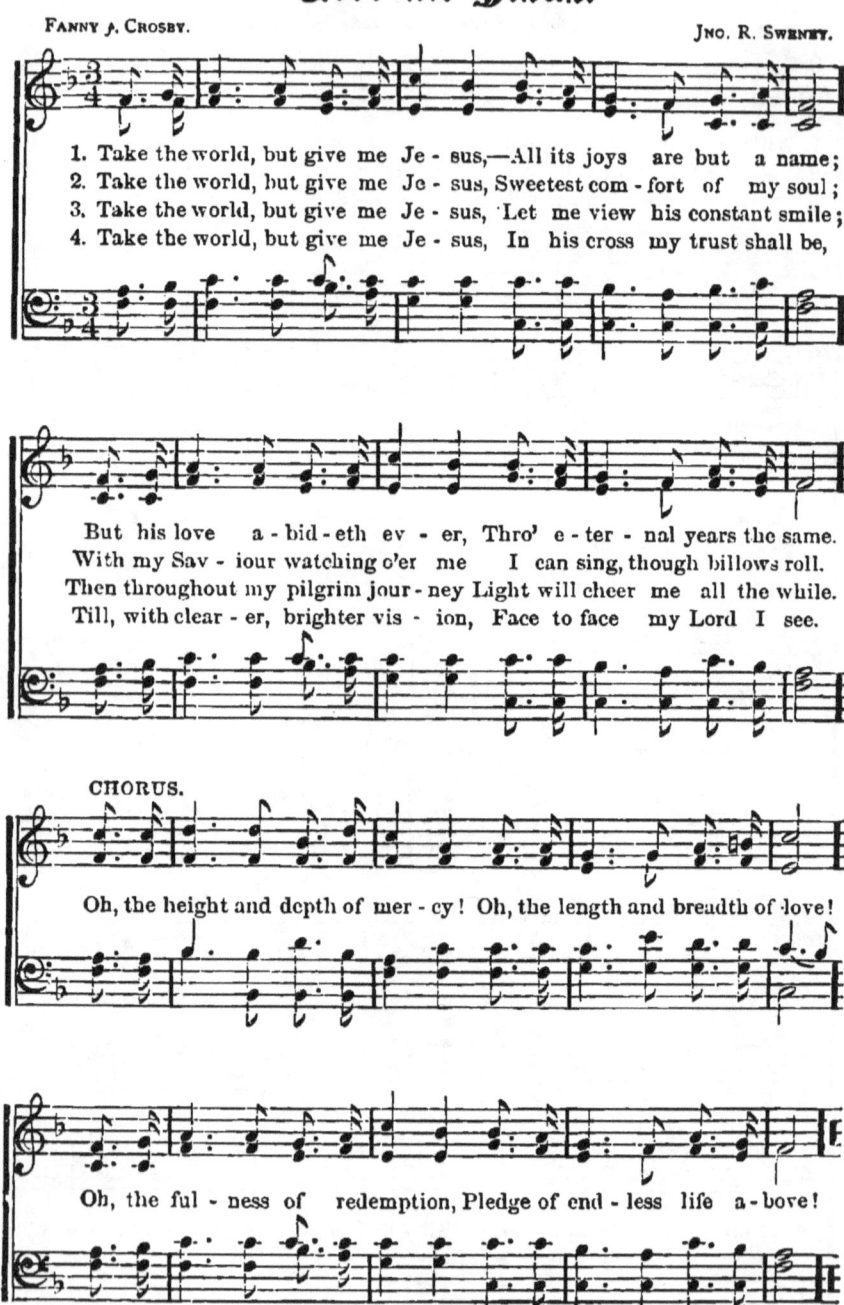

All the Way.—CONCLUDED.

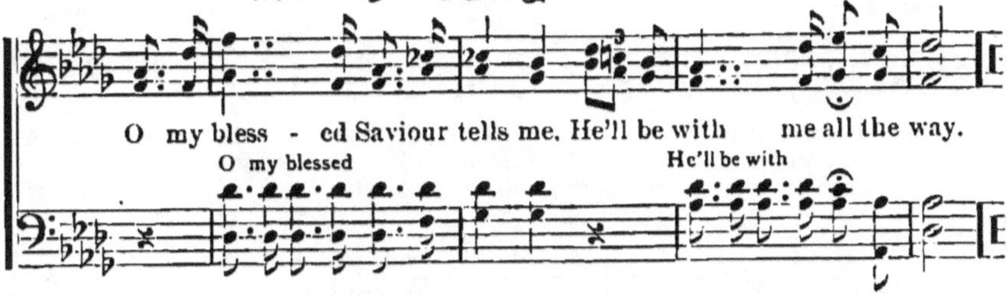

O my bless-ed Saviour tells me, He'll be with me all the way.
O my blessed   He'll be with

The Sweet New Name.

HARRIET E. JONES.   Rev. ii: 17.   J. HOWARD ENTWISLE.

1. A gold-en prom-ise I may claim, If true to God's dear Son:
2. O help me, Lord, to faithful prove That I may claim some day
3. Give me the strength to do thy will, Thro' days and years the same;

The se-cret name, the sweet new name,—Up-on a pure white stone.
This to-ken of thy ten-der love, To be my own for aye!
In weal or woe to serve thee still, At last, the promise claim.

CHORUS.

The sweet new name, the sweet new name, A gift from Christ, the Son!

O may I claim the sweet new name When earthly work is done. (is done.)

Copyright, 1899, by J. Howard Entwisle.

That Means Me.

Rev. Johnson Oatman, Jr. Adam Geibel.

1. I read that whoso-ev-er May from wrath flee; God will re-ject me never, For that means me.
2. His blood is ef-fi-cacious, His love is free; To sinners he is gracious, And that means me.

CHORUS.

For that means me, Yes, that means me; When I read "who-so-ev-er." Then that means me.

3 Christ died for every nation,
On Calv'ry's tree;
He died for our salvation,
And that means me.

4 I read the promise given,
That o'er death's sea,
We'll live with him in heaven,
And that means me.

Copyright, 1898, by J. Howard Entwisle.

Thinking of Home.

Rev. Johnson Oatman, Jr.
J. Howard Entwisle.

1. In that fair cit-y, over life's sea, There is a mansion waiting for me;
2. Father and mother gone to that shore, Home of my childhood open no more;
3. Brother and sister dwell in that land, Dear little rosebuds pluck'd from my hand;
4. O-ver the river soon I will glide, With the dear Saviour close to my side;

So on God's footstool tho' I may roam, All of the way I'm thinking of home.
Are they not watching over the foam, Waiting, while I am thinking of home?
Are not my lov'd ones beckoning come, Oh, do they know I'm thinking of home?
But till I reach that city's bright dome, I shall be always thinking of home.

CHORUS.

Thinking of home, yes, thinking of home, Beautiful home, my heavenly home;

Tho' from its portals long I may roam, All of the way I'm thinking of home.

Copyright, 1899, by J. Howard Entwisle.

4 Salvation why will you neglect?
  Why longer still do you reject
    The Holy Spirit's call?
  Oh, let it not of you be said
  These words so sad, when you are dead,
    "Lost after all, lost after all!"

5 Then come to Jesus, come just now,
  Low at his footstool humbly bow,
    He'll hear you when you call;
  Shall angels bear the joyful news?
  Or must they say, if you refuse,
    "Lost after all, lost after all?"

A Sinner Saved.—CONCLUDED. 71

And I'll tell forev-er How he saved when I came pleading before his feet.

Let Us Do What We Can.

IDA L. REED. W. T. DASHIELL.

1. Let us do what we can for Je-sus, While the bright hours glide away;
2. Let us do what we can with gladness, Tho' the service be but small;
3. Let us do what we can, unheed-ing What the world may think or say;

Let us toil for his glo-ry ev-er, Let us hope and trust and pray.
It may bright-en some one's sadness, Or some wand'rer's steps recall.
Let us follow his bless-ed leading, Cheer'd by love's unchanging ray.

CHORUS.

Let us do what we can for Je-sus, Who hath died our souls to save;

Let us work for his kingdom ev-er, And be faithful, true and brave.

Copyright, 1899, by Jno. R. Sweney.

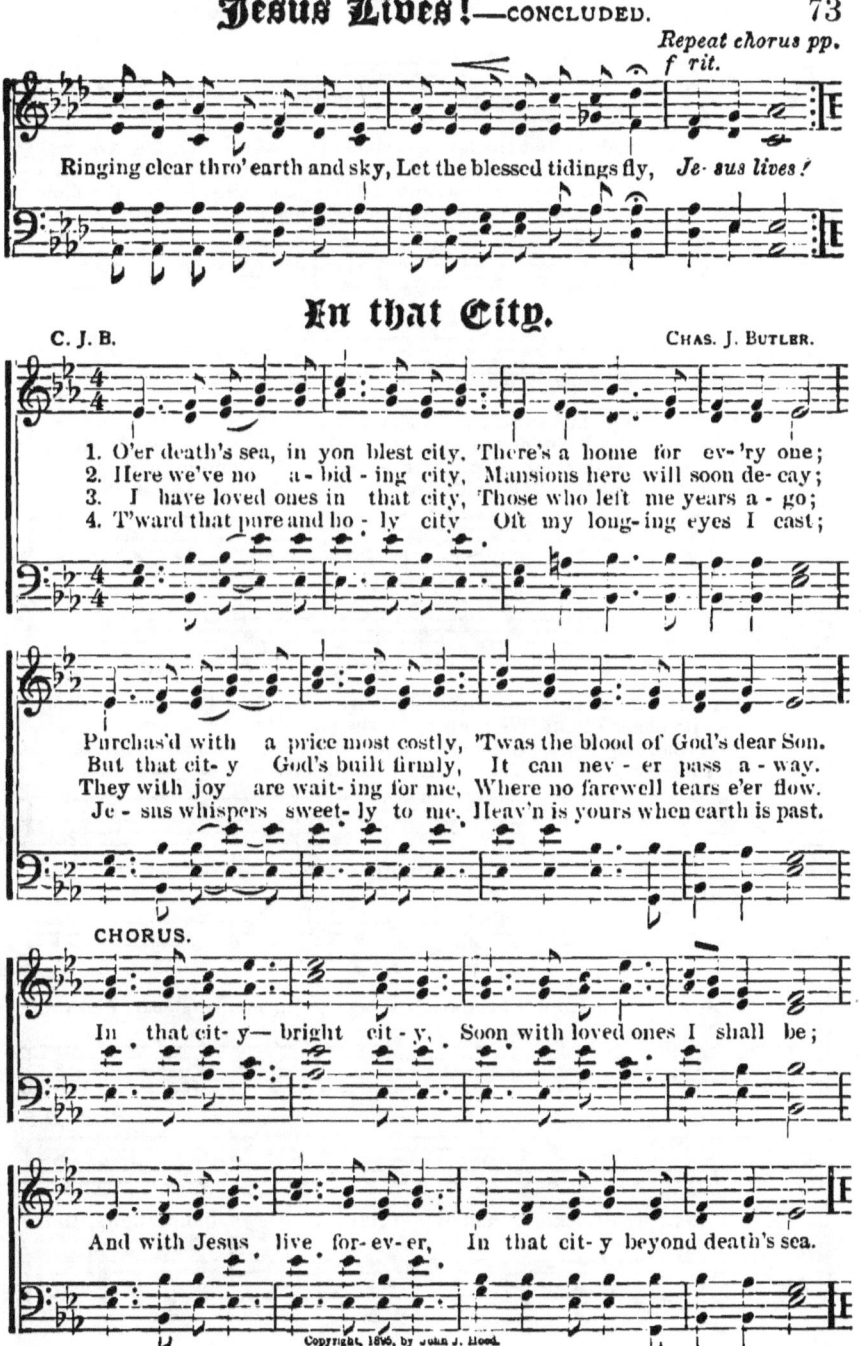

Sing On.—CONCLUDED. 77

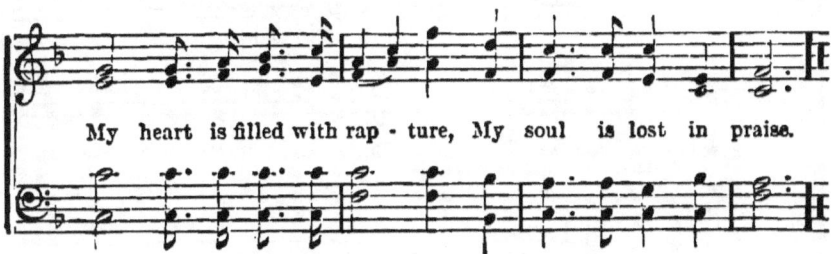

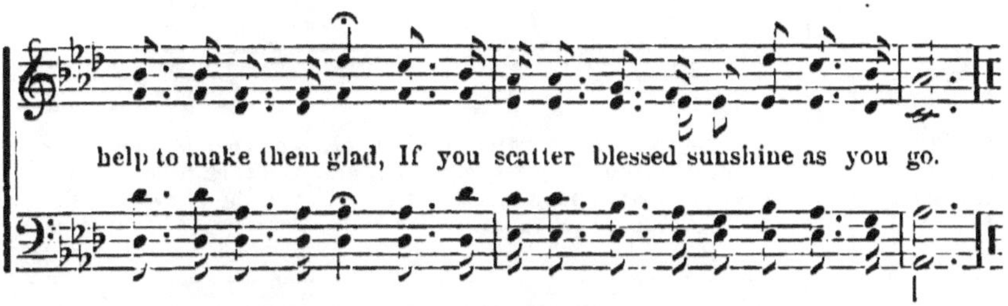

Sunshine as You Go.—CONCLUDED.

help to make them glad, If you scatter blessed sunshine as you go.

When Christ Arose.

IDA SCOTT TAYLOR. J. HOWARD ENTWISLE.

1. The earth was fill'd with peace and light, When Christ arose; The heavens trembled
2. The tomb was empty where he lay, When Christ arose; And angels roll'd the
3. The soul of man was born anew, When Christ arose; The cross divine ap-

at the sight, When Christ arose; The sea rejoiced along the sands, The vernal
stone away, When Christ arose; A sound of triumph thrill'd the air, The glorious
pear'd in view, When Christ arose; And from the
A glorious light from heaven stream'd,

valleys clapp'd their hands, The mountains sang, and all the lands, When Christ arose.
tidings to declare, And there was gladness ev'rywhere, When Christ arose.
cross a radiance beam'd, For ev-'ry spir- it was redeemed, When Christ arose.

Copyright, 1899, by J. Howard Entwisle.

Don't You Know He Cares? 81

Like Elijah, when he sat under the Juniper tree and prayed for the Lord to take his life, how often we in hours of trouble, sit under our Juniper tree of sorrow alone and cry out, "I am passing through the waters and 'Nobody Cares.'"

Rev. JOHNSON OATMAN, Jr.   J. HOWARD ENTWISLE.

1. When your spirit bows in sor - row / From the load it bears,
2. Have your feet become en- tang - led / In the tempter's snares?
3. Have you been by grief o'ertak - en, / Strick - en un - awares?
4. Is your bod - y filled with anguish, / With the pain it bears?

Go and tell your heart to Je - sus,— Don't you know he cares?
There is One who died to save you, Don't you know he cares?
Yet you will not be for - sak - en, Don't you know he cares?
Think of how the Saviour suf - fered— Don't you know he cares?

CHORUS.

Yes, there is One who shares your burdens, Ev - 'ry sor - row shares;

Go and tell it all to Je - sus,— Don't you know he cares?

Copyright, 1897, by John J. Hood.

5 Loss of friends and loss of fortune—
   Life a dark look wears;
   Yet the Saviour still is with you,
   Don't you know he cares?

6 So amid life's cares and struggles,
   Blending songs with prayers—
   Always put your trust in Jesus,
   Don't you know he cares?

Bright Melodies—F

82. The Beautiful, Beautiful Hills.

"I will lift up mine eyes unto the hills from whence cometh my help."—Ps. cxxi: 1.

Rev. Johnson Oatman, Jr. J. Howard Entwisle.

1. When my soul is oppress'd, When my heart is distress'd, With its weight of life's burdens and ills,— I will lift up mine eyes Un-to that par-a-dise On the beautiful, beautiful hills. On the hills, beautiful hills, I will lift up mine eyes to the hills; I shall join in the song With that glorified throng

2. That fair cit-y of God, Mortal never hath trod, There the cold wind of death nev-er chills; There no fears can appall, There no tears ev-er fall

3. There the angels of light Praise the Lord day and night, Heaven's courts with [their melody thrills, While there rolls a new song By that great blood-wash'd throng

D. S.—On the beautiful, beautiful hills.

4 Where my dear ones await,
  Just inside the pearl gate,
I shall go when my dear Father wills,
  Then what joy there will be,
  When each other we see
On the beautiful, beautiful hills.

5 There they never have night,
  For the Lamb is the light.—
All the land with his glory he fills:
  Soon he'll call me to come,
  And with him rest at home
On the beautiful, beautiful hills.

Copyright, 1899, by J. Howard Entwisle.

84. When Christ is In the Heart.

Rev. Johnson Oatman, Jr.   J. Howard Entwisle.

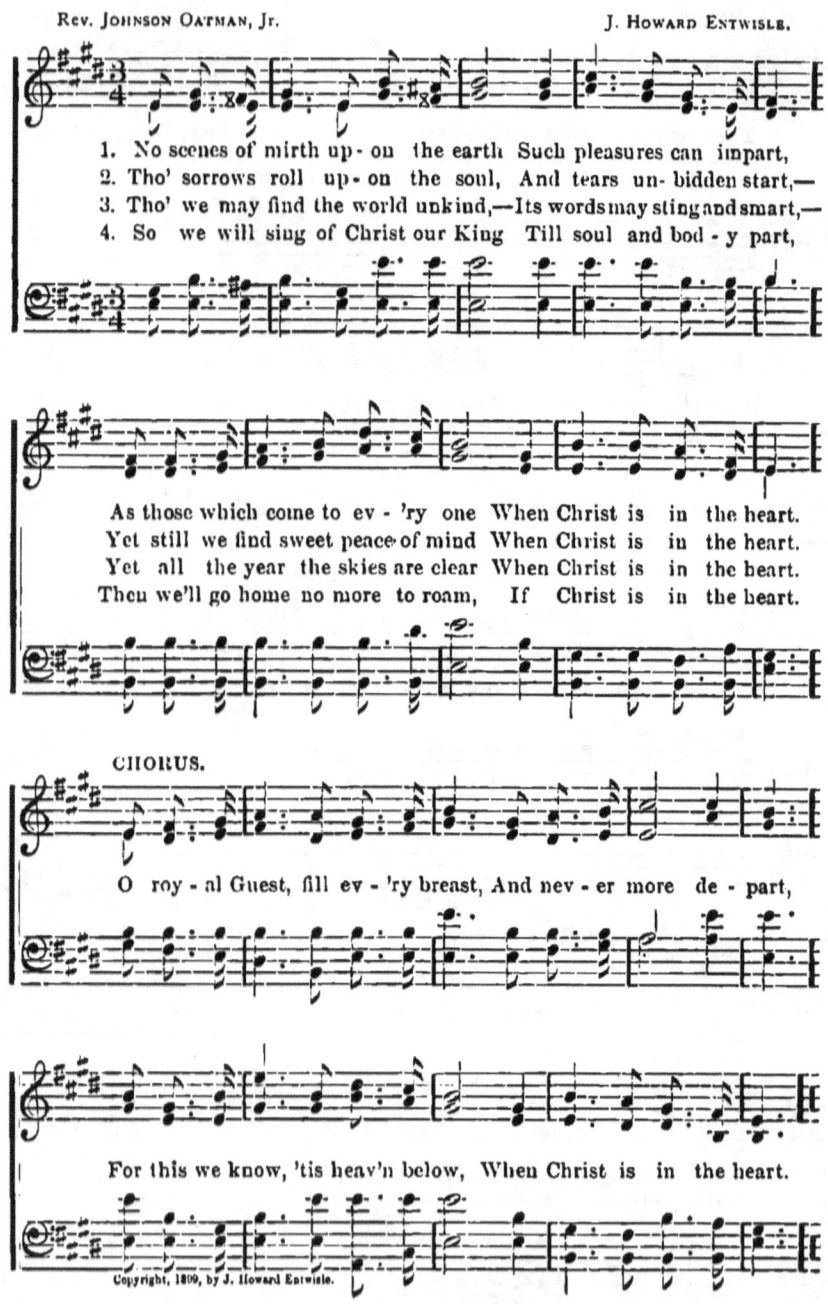

1. No scenes of mirth upon the earth Such pleasures can impart,
2. Tho' sorrows roll upon the soul, And tears unbidden start,—
3. Tho' we may find the world unkind,—Its words may sting and smart,—
4. So we will sing of Christ our King Till soul and body part,

As those which come to ev-'ry one When Christ is in the heart.
Yet still we find sweet peace of mind When Christ is in the heart.
Yet all the year the skies are clear When Christ is in the heart.
Then we'll go home no more to roam, If Christ is in the heart.

CHORUS.

O royal Guest, fill ev-'ry breast, And never more depart,
For this we know, 'tis heav'n below, When Christ is in the heart.

Copyright, 1899, by J. Howard Entwisle.

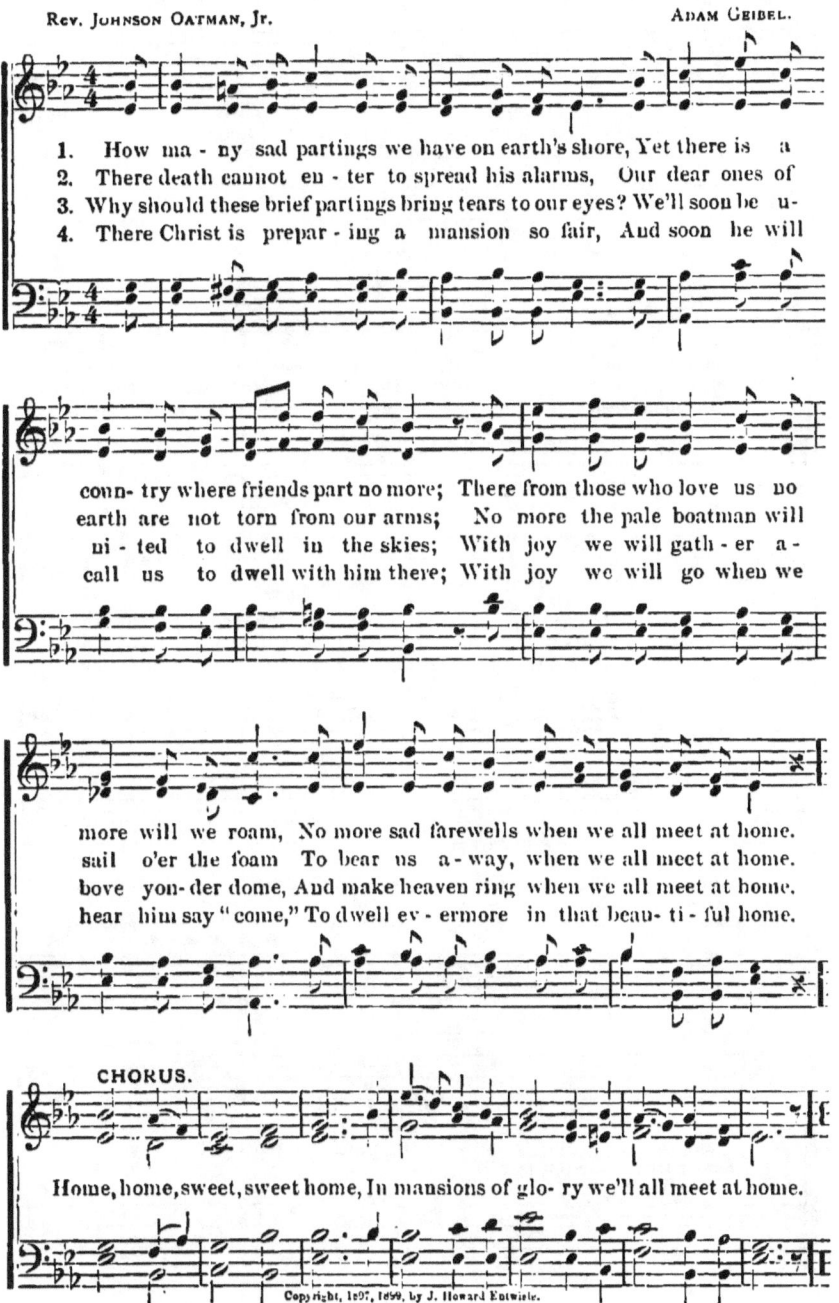

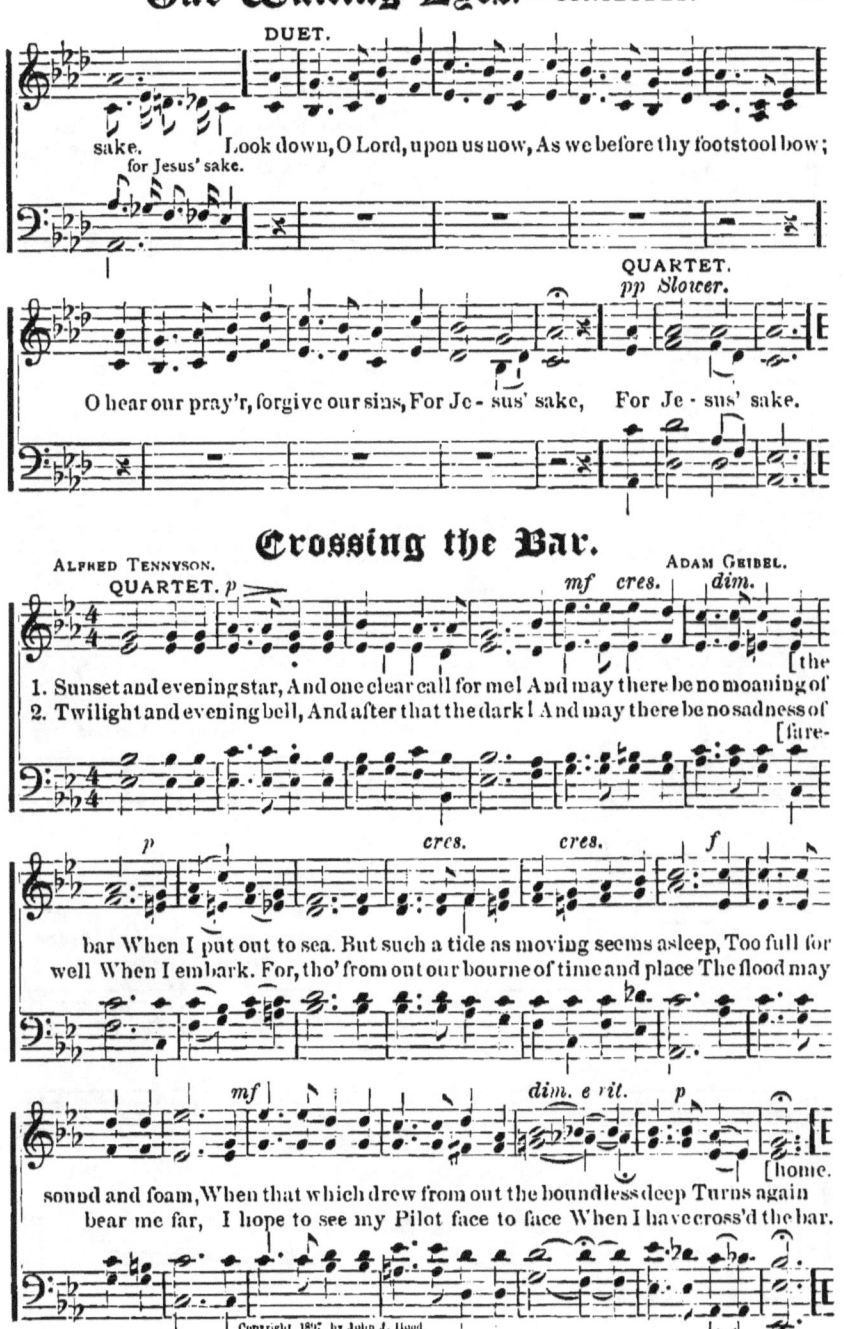

4 My yoke is easy,—burden light,
   Since Christ the Lord is mine!
   Each day my pathway seems more bright,
   Since Christ the Lord is mine!

5 In him I have each need supplied,
   Since Christ the Lord is mine!
   In him my soul is satisfied,
   Since Christ the Lord is mine!

The Lord Knoweth, etc.—CONCLUDED. 95

knoweth the way; Oh, let me to his hand cling fast Till earthly ills are o-verpast, And I shall reach his home at last, The Lord knoweth the way.

Jesus, Saviour, Pilot Me.

Rev. Edward Hopper.   J. E. Gould.

1. Je - sus, Saviour, pi - lot me, O - ver life's tempestuous sea;
2. As a moth- er stills her child, Thou canst hush the o - cean wild;
3. When at last I near the shore, And the fear - ful breakers roar

Unknown waves be- fore me roll, Hid- ing rock and treach'rous shoal;
Boist'rous waves o - bey thy will, When thou say'st to them "Be still!"
'Twixt me and the peaceful rest, Then, while leaning on thy breast,

Chart and compass come from thee: Je- sus, Sav- iour, pi - lot me.
Wondrous Sov'reign of the sea, Je - sus, Sav - iour, pi - lot me.
May I hear thee say to me, "Fear not, I will pi - lot thee!"

Far from the Fold.

J. H. E.
J. Howard Entwisle.

1. Far from the fold, how many sheep are straying, Out on the mountains, des-o-late and bare; Hungry and cold, with wea-ry feet they wander Far from the homeland and the Shepherd's care.
2. Who'll seek the lost? oh, who will follow Jesus, On thro' the night, nor heeding toil and pain? Who for *his sake* will prove a servant faithful— Bringing the wand'rer to the fold a-gain?
3. Sweet would it be, if you and I could answer, "Lord, I have sought thy sheep on mountains cold, Faithful to thee, at last, dear Lord, I've found one, Now it is safe-ly sheltered in thy fold.

CHORUS.

O come, let us go and seek the lost one, Wand'ring far on the mountains cold; 'Twill be sweet to say at the close of day, "I have brought one sheep to the fold."

Copyright, 1897, by John J. Hood.

Bright Melodies—G

4 Did ever saint find this friend forsake him?
No, not one! no, not one!
Or sinner find that he would not take him?
No, not one! no, not one!

5 Was e'er a gift like the Saviour given?
No, not one! no, not one!
Will he refuse us a home in heaven?
No, not one! no, not one!

Work in the Light.—CONCLUDED. 101

CHORUS.

Work in the light, be firm and true, Keeping our pledge forever in view; Eager to learn and ready to do our Lord's command; Lifting the soul oppress'd into the calm of rest, Heeding the call that speaks to all, go, work to-day. . . . .

My Country! 'Tis of Thee.

S. F. SMITH.   Tune, AMERICA. 6, 4.

1. My country! 'tis of thee, Sweet land of liberty, Of thee I sing; Land where my
2. My native country, thee, Land of the noble, free, Thy name I love; I love thy
3. Let music swell the breeze, And ring from all the trees
                                            [Sweet freedom's song; Let mortal
4. Our Father's God, to thee, Author of liberty, To thee we sing; Long may our

cres.

father's died! Land of the pilgrim's pride! From ev'ry mountain side Let freedom ring.
rocks and rills, Thy woods and templed hills;   [My heart with rapture thrills, Like that above.
tongues awake,   [Let all that breathe partake, Let rocks their silence break, The sound prolong.
land be bright With freedom's holy light; Protect us by thy might, Great God, our
                                                                                               [King.

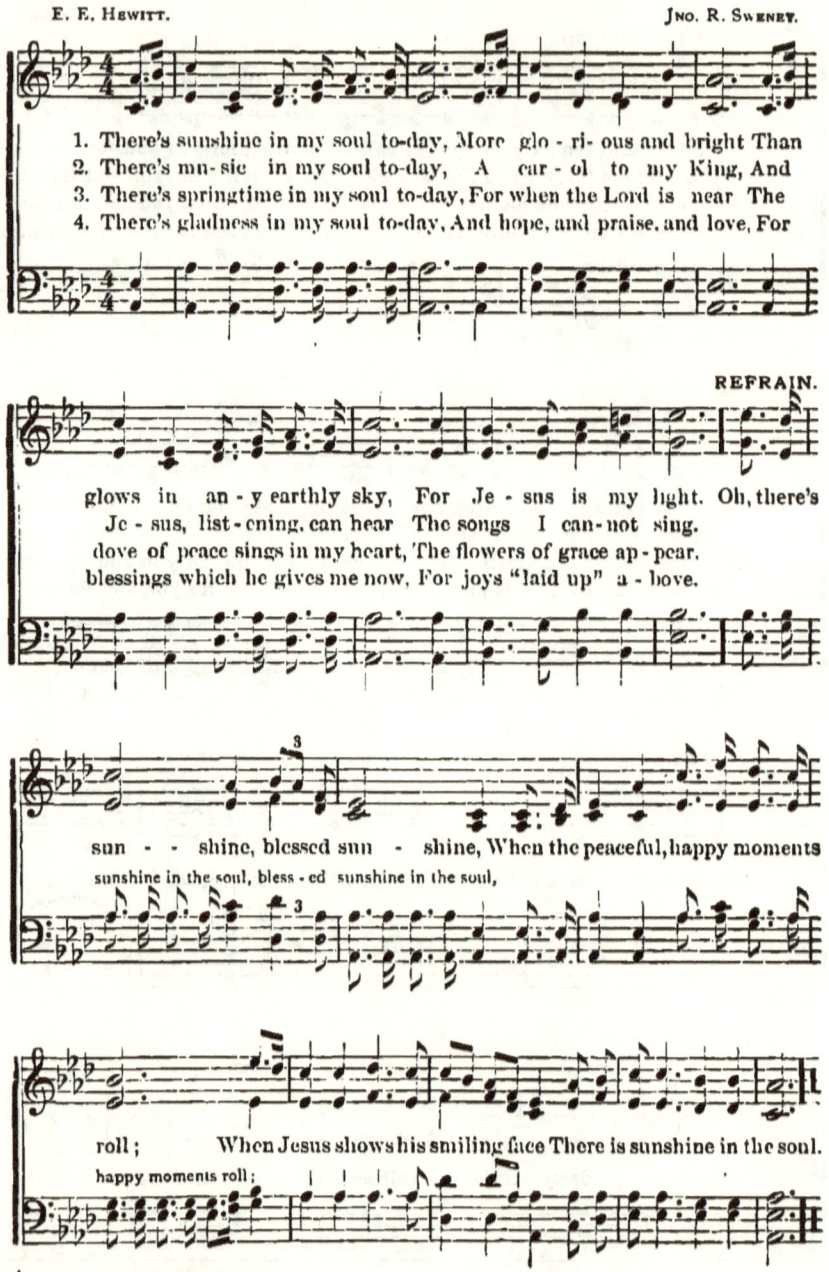

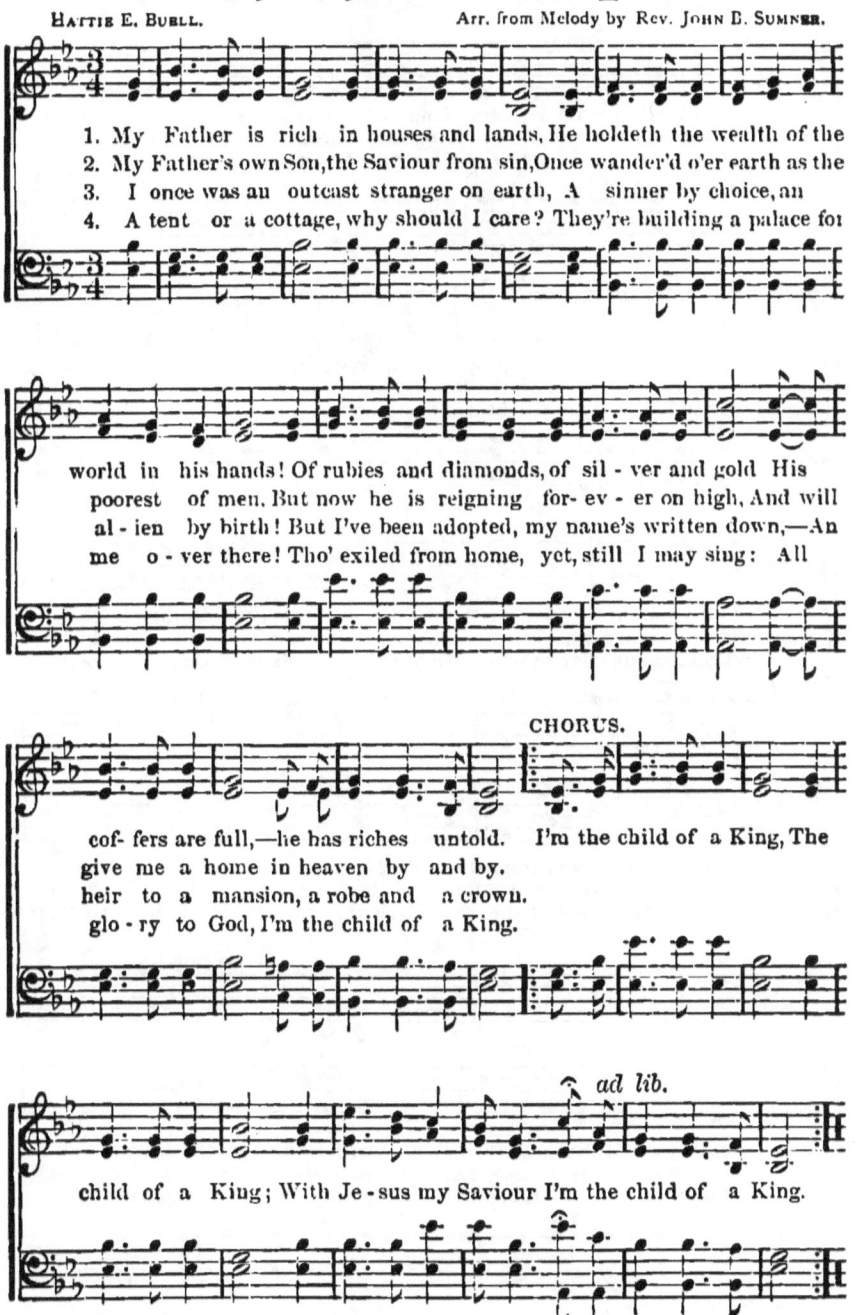

Journey in the King's, etc.—CONCLUDED. 109

Come, in shining robes be clad, And go singing in the King's highway.

Holy Spirit, Heavenly Dove.

Rev. Johnson Oatman, Jr.   J. Howard Entwisle.

1. Ho-ly Spir-it from a-bove, Fill each bos-om with thy love;
2. Come, thou Ho-ly Com-fort-er, Wilt thou not this boon con-fer?
3. We have full sur-ren-der made, All is on the al-tar laid,

Come with pow'r our souls to greet, Meet us at the mer-cy seat.
En-ter ev-'ry trembling breast, May each soul find per-fect rest.
With thy sac-ri-fi-cial flame Now ac-cept it in thy name.

CHORUS.

Ho-ly Spir-it, Heav'nly Dove, Fill us with thy per-fect love,

In our hearts all dross re-fine, Till thine im-age there may shine.

Copyright, 1899, by J. Howard Entwisle.

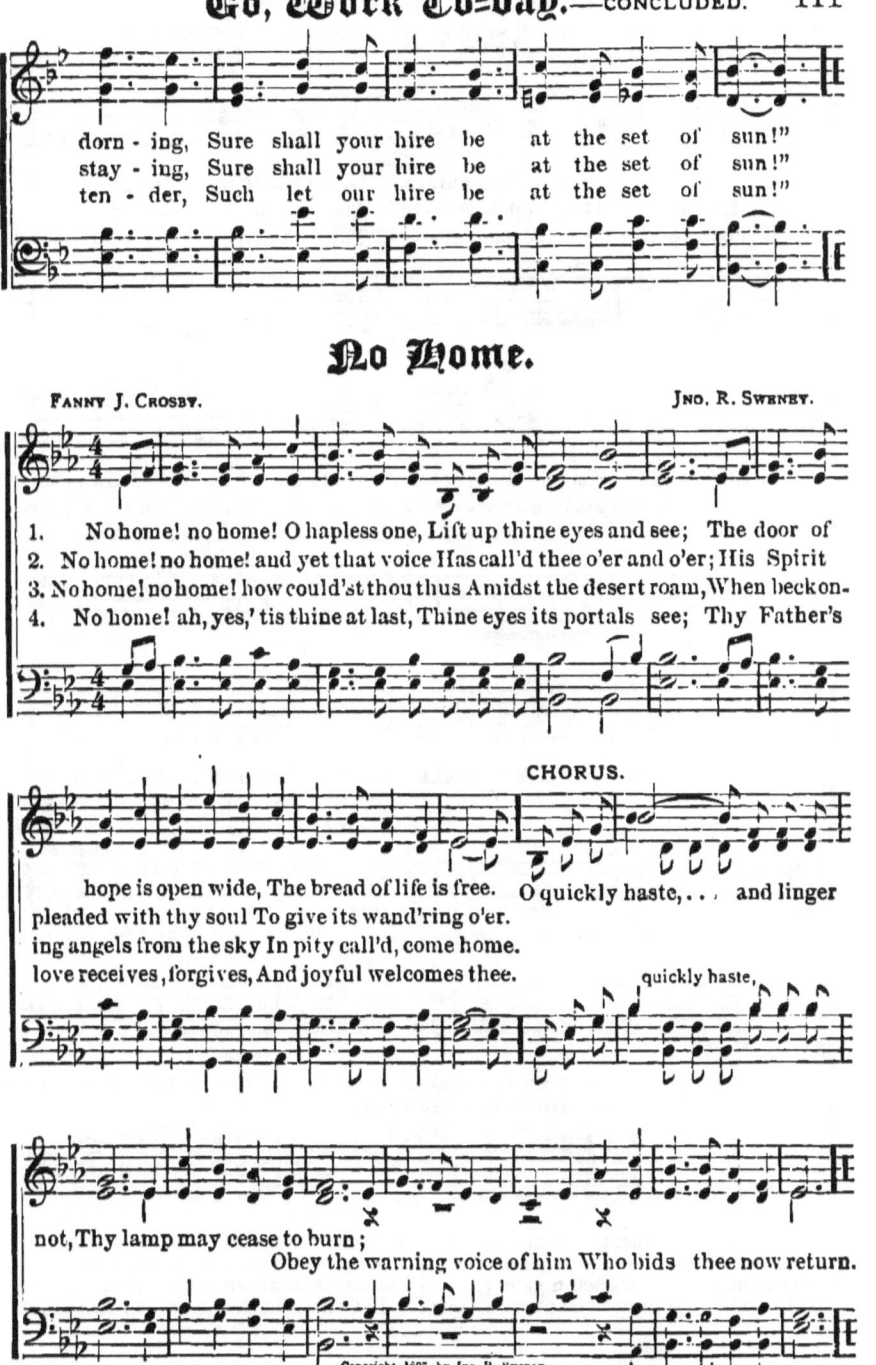

In God's Own Time.

112

"And let us not be weary in well doing: for in due season we shall reap, if we faint not."—Gal. vi: 9.

Rev. Johnson Oatman, Jr.
J. Howard Entwisle.

SOLO OR DUET

1. If o'er thy way dark clouds are cast, Look up with faith till they are past, The sun will surely shine at last, In God's own time, in God's own time.
2. Hast thou pray'd long and fervent-ly, And yet no an-swer came to thee? Thy pray'r will sometime answer'd be, In God's own time, in God's own time.
3. Look up with joy, nor long-er weep, Thy God will ev-'ry promise keep, And thou wilt yet the harvest reap, In God's own time, in God's own time.

CHORUS.

Then do not fear, tho' dark the night, But rise on wings of faith sublime,
rise on wings of faith sublime,
Do not fear, tho' dark the night, rise on wings, on wings of faith sublime.

rit.

For ev'rything will come out right, In God's own time, in God's own time.
yes, ev'rything will come out right, In God's own time.

Copyright, 1898, by J. Howard Entwisle.

4 Tho' thro' the glass thou can'st not see,
And wonder why some things must be,
Yet thou wilt know each mystery,
In God's own time, in God's own time.

5 And would'st thou be forever blest?
Just trust in God and do thy best,
Then thou shalt enter into rest,
In God's own time, in God's own time.

Wonderful Peace.

L. H. E.   "My peace I give unto you."—John xiv: 27.   L. H. Edmunds.

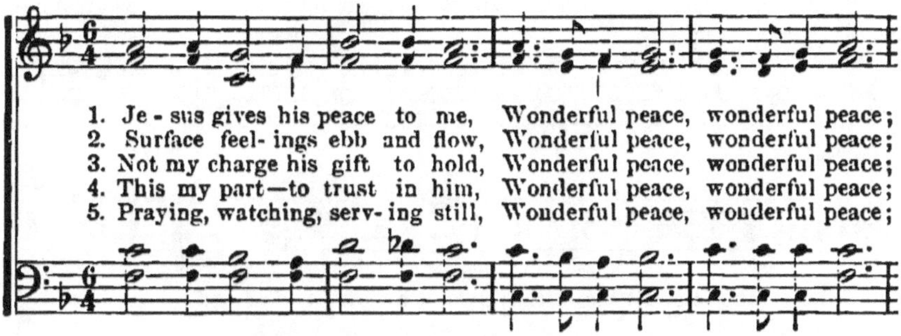

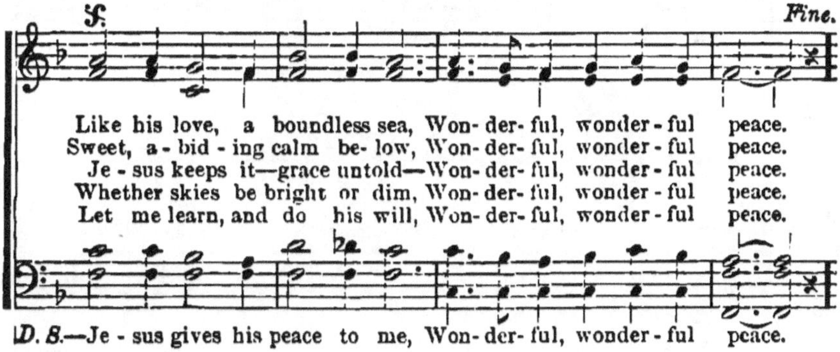

1. Je-sus gives his peace to me, Wonderful peace, wonderful peace;
2. Surface feel-ings ebb and flow, Wonderful peace, wonderful peace;
3. Not my charge his gift to hold, Wonderful peace, wonderful peace;
4. This my part—to trust in him, Wonderful peace, wonderful peace;
5. Praying, watching, serv-ing still, Wonderful peace, wonderful peace;

Like his love, a boundless sea, Won-der-ful, wonder-ful peace.
Sweet, a-bid-ing calm be-low, Won-der-ful, wonder-ful peace.
Je-sus keeps it—grace untold—Won-der-ful, wonder-ful peace.
Whether skies be bright or dim, Won-der-ful, wonder-ful peace.
Let me learn, and do his will, Won-der-ful, wonder-ful peace.

D. S.—Je-sus gives his peace to me, Won-der-ful, wonder-ful peace.

REFRAIN.

Peace, peace, won-der-ful peace, Peace, peace, won-der-ful peace;

Copyright, 1896, by John J. Hood.

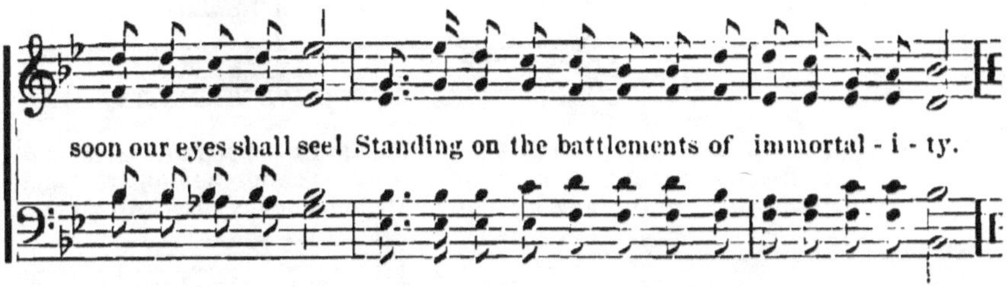

Standing On, etc.—CONCLUDED.

soon our eyes shall see! Standing on the battlements of immortal-i-ty.

Neither Do I Condemn Thee.

F. M. D.   "Go, and sin no more."—John viii: 11.   Frank M. Davis.

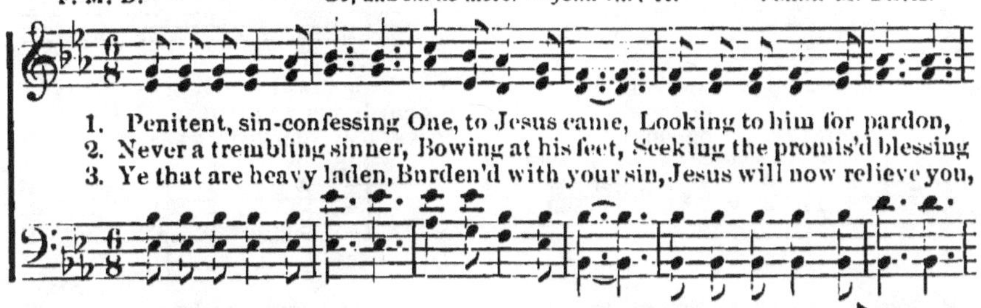

1. Penitent, sin-confessing One, to Jesus came, Looking to him for pardon,
2. Never a trembling sinner, Bowing at his feet, Seeking the promis'd blessing
3. Ye that are heavy laden, Burden'd with your sin, Jesus will now relieve you,

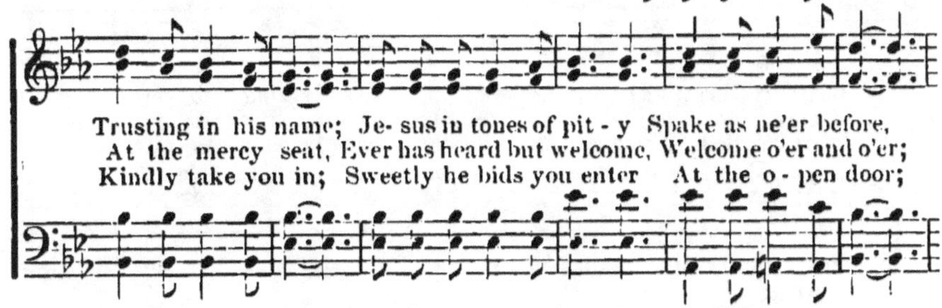

Trusting in his name; Jesus in tones of pit-y Spake as ne'er before,
At the mercy seat, Ever has heard but welcome, Welcome o'er and o'er;
Kindly take you in; Sweetly he bids you enter At the o-pen door;

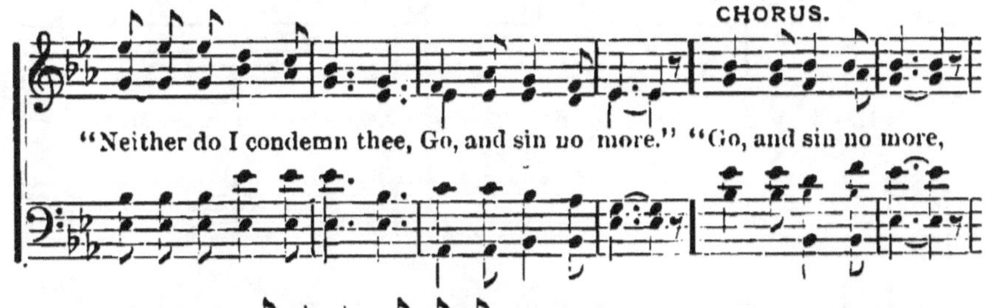

CHORUS.

"Neither do I condemn thee, Go, and sin no more." "Go, and sin no more,

Go, and sin no more; Neither do I condemn thee, Go, and sin no more."

From "Brightest Glory." By per. of John J. Hood.

120   What a Joyous Time!

Ida Scott Taylor.   J. Howard Entwisle.

1. What a joyous time to meet And our love to Christ repeat, Great and small, one and all; While the hours are passing by Ev'ry heart is beating high, As we sing, sweetly sing to our King.
2. What a friendship true and warm Christ's beloved children form, Great and small, one and all; How our tongues united swell His redeeming love to tell, As we sing, sweetly sing to our King.
3. Tender thoughts we give to each, Kindly smiles and loving speech, Great and small, one and all; When we meet from year to year, May each heart be filled with cheer, As we sing, sweetly sing to our King.

D.S.—heart is beating high, As we sing, sweetly sing to our King.

CHORUS.

Happy day, happy day, Tho' you hasten now away, May your joy with us stay, happy day; While the hours are passing by, Ev'ry

Copyright, 1898, by J. Howard Entwisle.

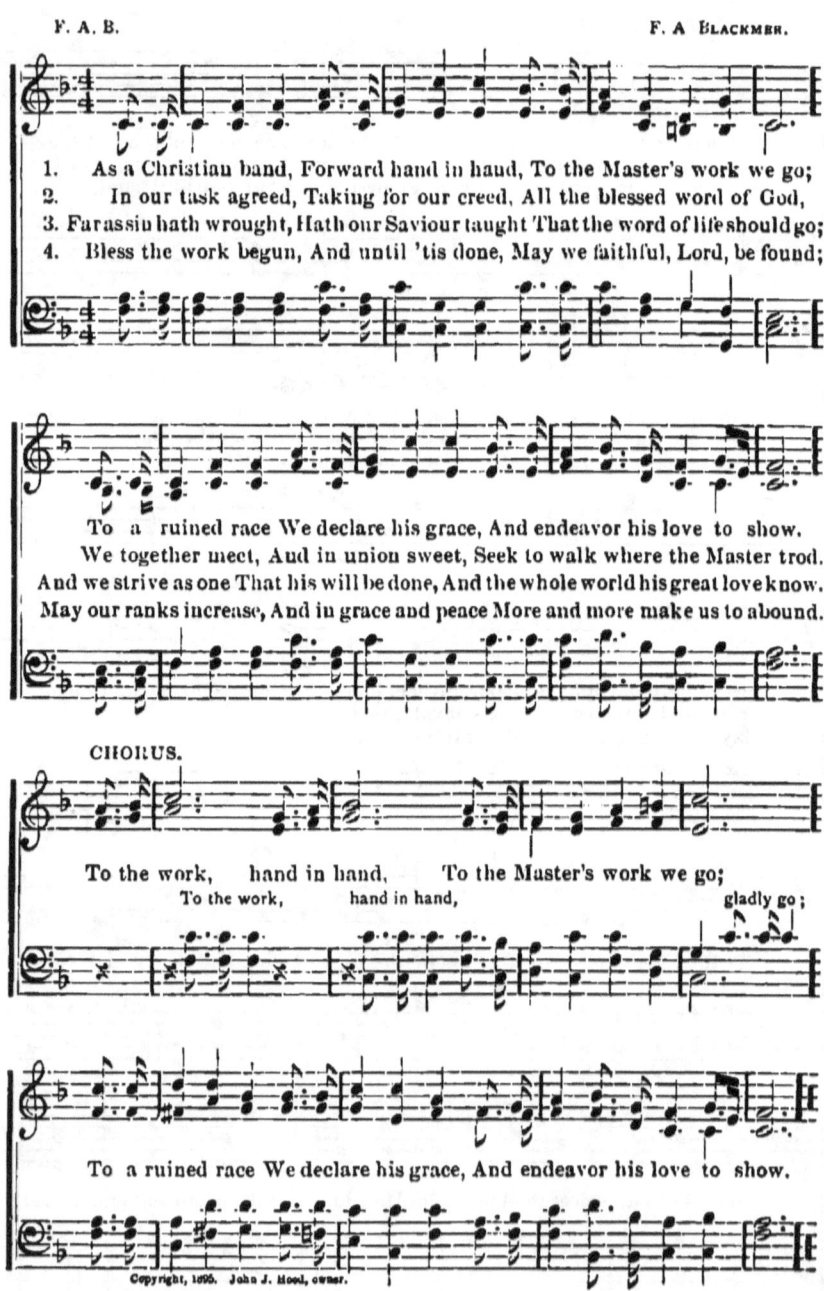

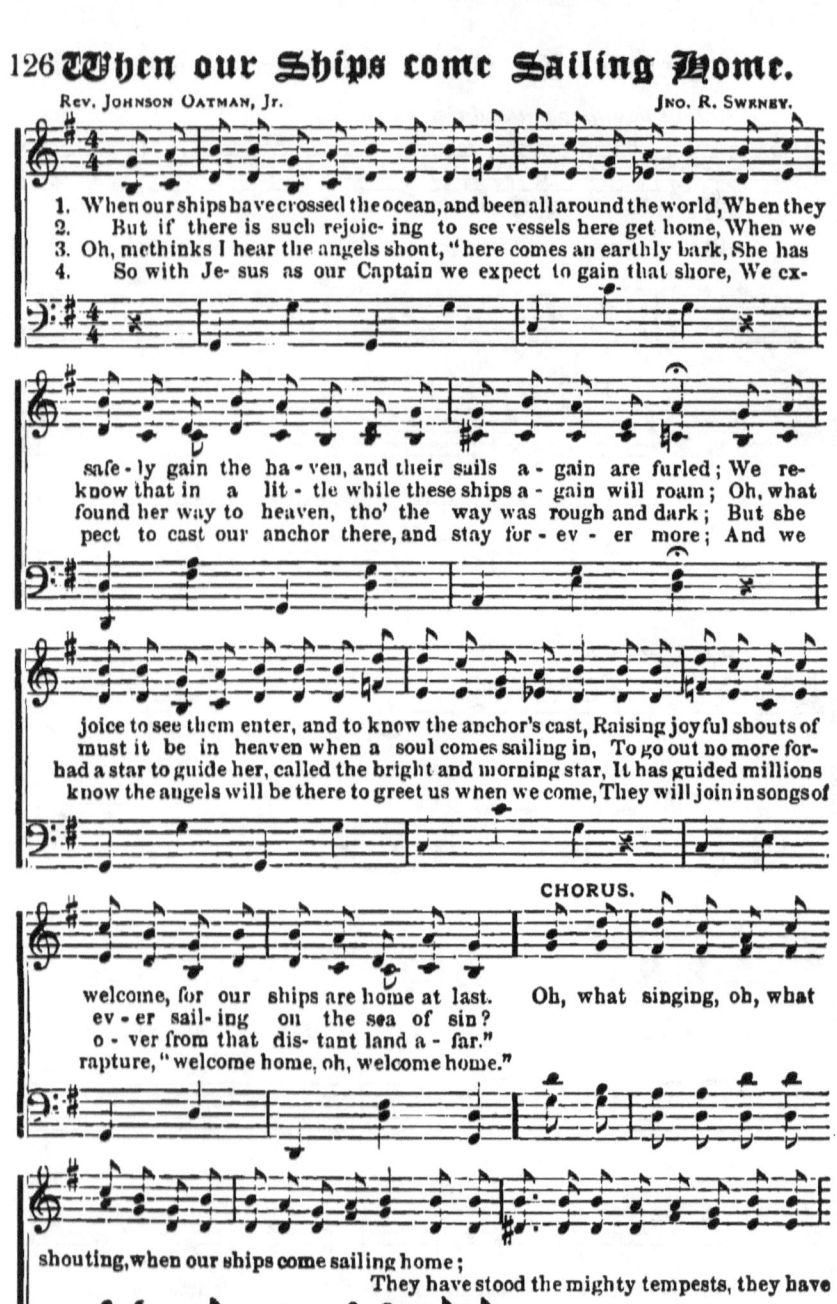

When our Ships, etc.—CONCLUDED.

crossed the o-cean's foam; They have passed o'er stormy billows, but they now have gained the shore, The anchor's cast, they're home at last, the voyage is safely [o'er.

Abide with Me.

HENRY F. LYTE.   Tune, EVENTIDE. 10s.

1. Abide with me! fast falls the eventide, The darkness deepens—Lord, with me abide! When other helpers fail, and comforts flee, Help of the helpless, oh, abide with me.

2 Swift to its close ebbs out life's little day;
Earth's joys grow dim, its glories pass away;
Change and decay in all around I see;
O thou, who changest not, abide with me!

3 I need thy presence every passing hour;
What but thy grace can foil the tempter's power?
Who, like thyself, my guide and stay can be?
Through cloud and sunshine, Lord, abide with me!

4 I fear no foe, with thee at hand to bless;
Ills have no weight, and tears no bitterness;
Where is death's sting? where, grave, thy victory?
I triumph still, if thou abide with me.

5 Hold thou thy cross before my closing eyes;
Shine through the gloom and point me to the skies;
Heaven's morning breaks, and earth's vain shadows flee;
In life, in death, O Lord, abide with me!

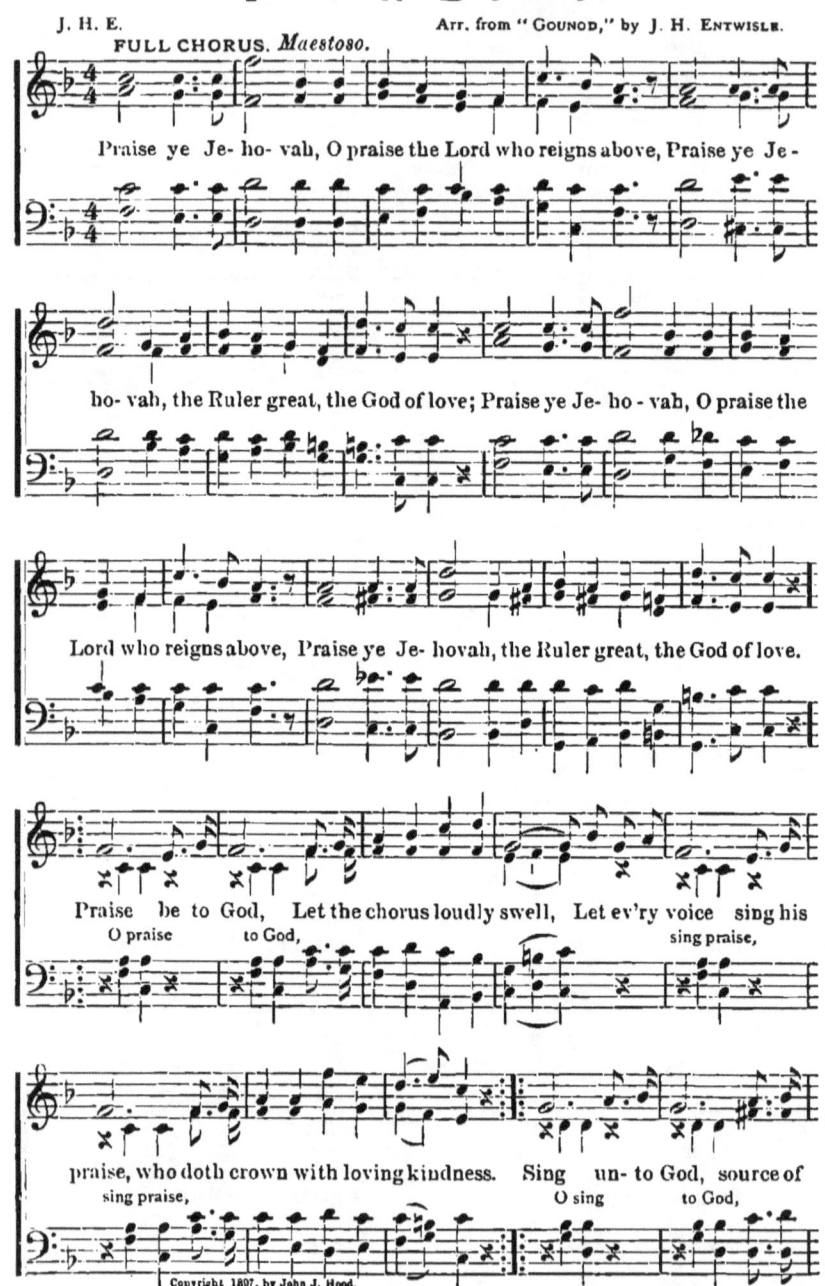

Praise Ye Jehovah.—CONCLUDED. 131

* Use small notes if desirable.

132. See! They are Drifting.

"Cry aloud! ... lift up thy voice like a trumpet!" —Isa. lviii : 1.

Mrs. Harriet E. Jones.   J. Howard Entwisle.

With great expression.

1. Out on sin's o-cean the careless are drifting, Far from the beacon that leadeth a-right; Servants of Je-sus, your voi-ces be lift-ing, Calling them back from the darkness of night.
2. Darkness and danger are surely before them, Farther and farther they're drifting a-way; Forward! my brothers, to warn and implore them, Call them to Je-sus, lest farther they stray.
3. Call to them, brothers, their barks to be turning, Point to the beacon of safe-ty and light; Point to the bea-con for wan-der-ers burn-ing, Lighting the pathway to E-den-land bright.

CHORUS.

See! they are drifting, *your* brothers are drifting, See! they are tossing on sin's dreadful wave! Like to a trumpet your voices be lifting, Call them to Je-sus, the mighty to save.

Copyright, 1897, by John J. Hood.

The Lord is Our Refuge.

133

Mrs. S. L. Oberholtzer.
Adam Geibel.

1. The Lord is our refuge, Our fortress and power, His strength will defend us
2. The Lord our protector, Our strength and our might, Will never forsake us
3. The Lord is our gladness, The Lord is our King, He guards us and guides us,

In life's darkest hour, His love all-suf-fi-cient Will fill ev-'ry need,
By day or by night; His care is around us, His mer-cy is free,
If we to him cling, The Lord will de-liv-er, Will comfort and bless,

CHORUS.

His love ev-er-last-ing Is our life indeed. The Lord is our refuge,
His love that has found us Is be-yond degree.
And ev-er his children Are free from distress.

And we trust in him; The Lord is our sunshine That never grows dim.

Copyright, 1899, by John J. Hood.

The Pillar of Cloud.

"Yet thou in thy manifold mercies forsookest them not in the wilderness; the pillar of the cloud departed not from them by day, to lead them in the way; neither the pillar of fire by night, to show them light, and the way wherein they should go." — Neh. ix: 19.

F. A. B.   F. A. Blackmer.

1. On thy journey to the homeland, God is watching o-ver thee;
2. He that watches o-ver Is-rael, Nev-er slumbers, nev-er sleeps;
3. Forward then with courage, Christian, Light shall dawn from heaven's throne;
4. On the mountain, in the val-ley, Ev-'rywhere shall he sus-tain;

He shall light thy path, O trav'ler, Till thou canst the landmarks see.
And o'er all his faith-ful children Vig-i-lance e-ter-nal keeps.
He who set thee on thy journey Will not let thee walk a-lone.
And when darkness gathers round thee, Bring thee in-to light a-gain.

CHORUS.

The pillar of cloud shall go before thee, To guide thy footsteps day by day;

The pillar of fire shall shine before thee, And ev'ry night make clear thy way.

Copyright, 1894, 1899, by John J. Hood.

136. When we Reach our Home.

HARRIET E. JONES. J. HOWARD ENTWISLE.

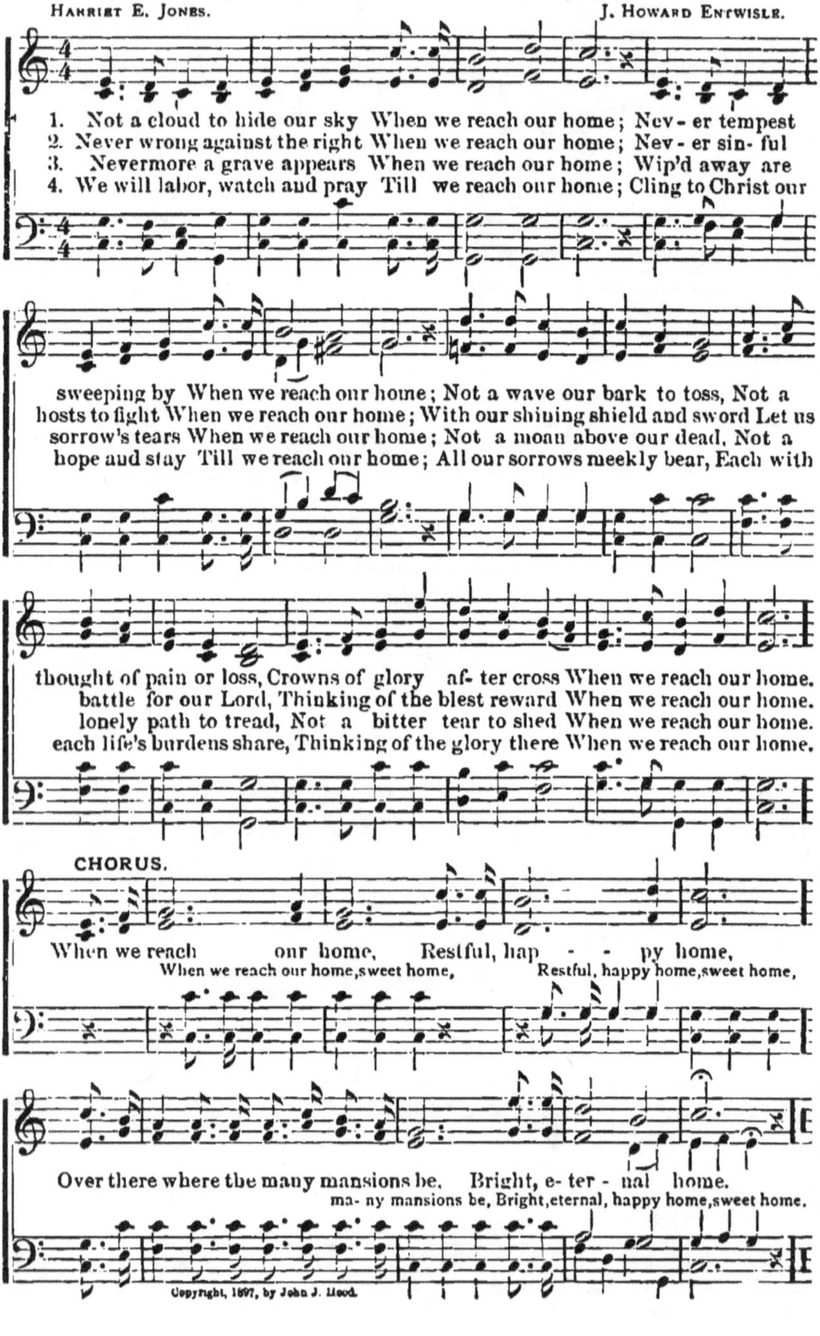

1. Not a cloud to hide our sky When we reach our home; Nev- er tempest
2. Never wrong against the right When we reach our home; Nev- er sin- ful
3. Nevermore a grave appears When we reach our home; Wip'd away are
4. We will labor, watch and pray Till we reach our home; Cling to Christ our

sweeping by When we reach our home; Not a wave our bark to toss, Not a
hosts to fight When we reach our home; With our shining shield and sword Let us
sorrow's tears When we reach our home; Not a moan above our dead, Not a
hope and stay Till we reach our home; All our sorrows meekly bear, Each with

thought of pain or loss, Crowns of glory af- ter cross When we reach our home.
battle for our Lord, Thinking of the blest reward When we reach our home.
lonely path to tread, Not a bitter tear to shed When we reach our home.
each life's burdens share, Thinking of the glory there When we reach our home.

CHORUS.

When we reach our home, Restful, hap - - py home,
When we reach our home, sweet home, Restful, happy home, sweet home,

Over there where the many mansions be. Bright, e- ter- nal home.
ma- ny mansions be, Bright, eternal, happy home, sweet home.

Copyright, 1897, by John J. Hood.

Just One Touch.

Birdie Bell.   J. Howard Entwisle.

SOLO. *Slow, with expression.*

1. Just one touch as he moves along, Push'd and press'd by the jostling throng,
2. Just one touch and he makes me whole, Speaks sweet peace to my sin-sick soul,
3. Just one touch! and the work is done, I am saved by the blessed Son,
4. Just one touch! and he turns to me, O the love in his eyes I see!
5. Just one touch! by his mighty pow'r, He can heal thee this ver-y hour,

Just one touch and the weak was strong, Cured by the Healer di-vine.
At his feet all my burdens roll,—Cured by the Healer di-vine.
I will sing while the a-ges run, Cured by the Healer di-vine.
I am his for he hears my plea, Cured by the Healer di-vine.
Thou canst hear tho' the tempests low'r, Cured by the Healer di-vine.

CHORUS.

Just one touch as he pass-es by, He will list to the faintest cry,

Come and be saved while the Lord is nigh, Christ is the Healer di-vine.

Copyright, 1897, by J. Howard Entwisle.

Waft, Ye Winds, etc.—CONCLUDED.

And tell them Christ the only Son, Hath died to make them free....
And tell ... to make them free.

Come, Come To-day.

Rev. Johnson Oatman, Jr.   J. Howard Entwisle.

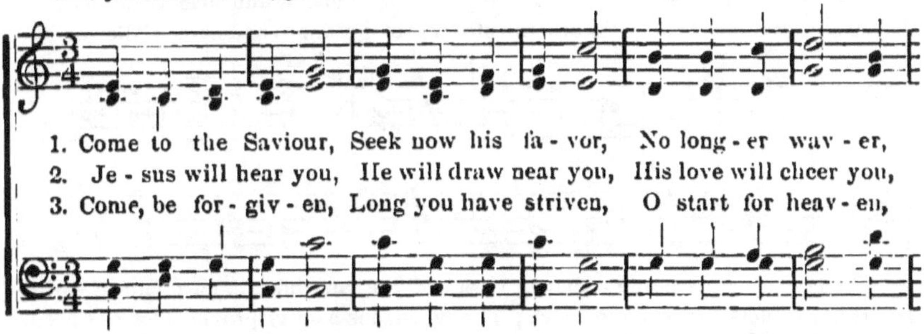

1. Come to the Saviour, Seek now his fa-vor, No long-er wav-er,
2. Je-sus will hear you, He will draw near you, His love will cheer you,
3. Come, be for-giv-en, Long you have striven, O start for heav-en,

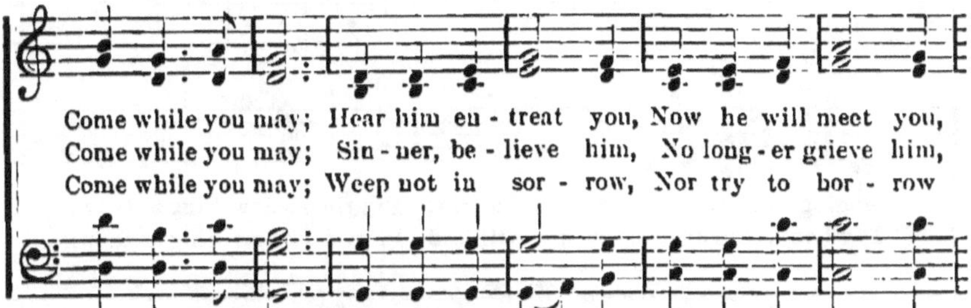

Come while you may; Hear him en-treat you, Now he will meet you,
Come while you may; Sin-ner, be-lieve him, No long-er grieve him,
Come while you may; Weep not in sor-row, Nor try to bor-row

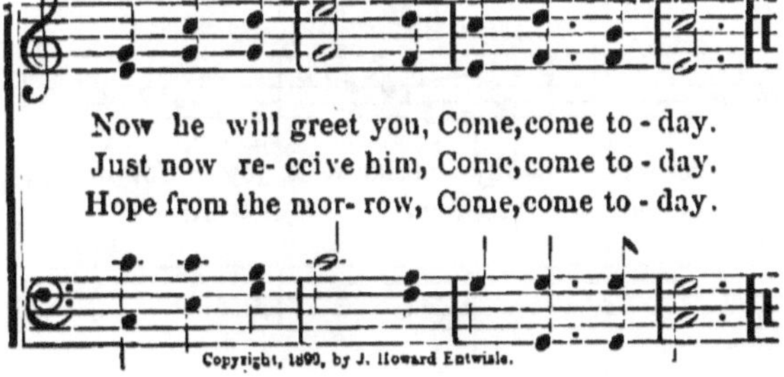

Now he will greet you, Come, come to-day.
Just now re-ceive him, Come, come to-day.
Hope from the mor-row, Come, come to-day.

4 Prayers are ascending,
Angels are bending,
Friends are attending,
   Come while you may;
Ere you are lying
Low with the dying,
For mercy crying,
   Come, come to-day.

Copyright, 1890, by J. Howard Entwisle.

Joyful Praises.—CONCLUDED.

Angel bands are singing; Joy - ful praises, joy - ful praises, We thy
Praise to thee, praise to thee,

children bringing; Joy - ful praises, joy - ful praises, Hearts and voices
Praise to thee, praise to thee,

ringing; Joy - ful praises, joy - ful praises, Lord, we give to thee.
Praise to thee, praise to thee,

The Lord is my Shepherd.

A - men.

1 The Lord is my Shepherd; I | shall not | want. ‖ He maketh me to lie down in green pastures: He leadeth me beside the still | wa- | ters.

2 He restoreth my soul: He leadeth me in the paths of righteousness for his | name's | sake. ‖ Yea, though I walk through the valley of the shadow of death, I will fear no evil: for thou art with me; thy rod and thy staff they | comfort | me.

3 Thou preparest a table before me in the presence of mine enemies: Thou anointest my head with oil; my | cup runneth | over. ‖ Surely goodness and mercy shall follow me all the days of my life: And I will dwell in the house of the Lord for- | ev- | er. ‖ A- | men.

144. Bought on Calvary.

HARRIET E. JONES. J. HOWARD ENTWISLE.

m With much expression.

1. There is a beau-ti-ful home Beyond the si-lent sea,
2. There is a beau-ti-ful house To stand e-ter-nal-ly,
3. There is a beau-ti-ful robe As white as white can be,
4. There is a beau-ti-ful crown To ev-er fade-less be,
5. These beauti-ful gifts of love That wait be-yond the sea,

And oh, that home so bright and fair My Sav-iour bought for me.
And oh, that house not made with hands My Sav-iour bought for me.
And oh, that robe so spotless, pure, My Sav-iour bought for me.
And oh, that wondrous crown of life My Sav-iour bought for me.
My Saviour purchas'd with his blood On cross of Cal-va-ry.

CHORUS.

O wand'rer, far from God, That home your own may be, If
O wand'rer, far from God, A mansion yours may be, If
O wand'rer, far from God, White raiment yours may be, If
O wand'rer, far from God, A crown your own may be, If
O wand'rer, far from God, This wealth your own may be, If
    wan-d'rer, far from God,

you will give your heart to Christ, And serve him, serve him faithful-ly.
you will give your heart to Christ, And serve him, serve him faithful-ly.
you will give your heart to Christ, And serve him, serve him faithful-ly.
you will give your heart to Christ, And serve him, serve him faithful-ly.
you will give your heart to Christ, And oh, 'tis free! and oh, 'tis free!

Copyright, 1897, by J. Howard Entwisle.

Praise the Lord, etc.—CONCLUDED.

lujah, ... Halle- lujah, ... Hallelujah, hallelujah, praise the Lord!
praise the Lord!   praise the Lord!

Love Lightens Burdens.

HARRIET E. JONES.   J. HOWARD ENTWISLE.

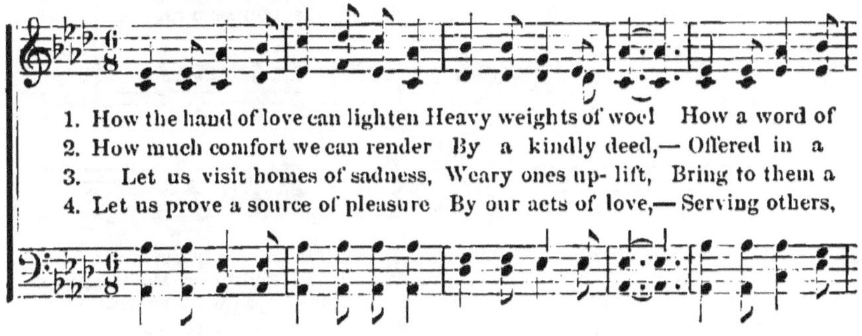

1. How the hand of love can lighten Heavy weights of woe! How a word of
2. How much comfort we can render By a kindly deed,— Offered in a
3. Let us visit homes of sadness, Weary ones up-lift, Bring to them a
4. Let us prove a source of pleasure By our acts of love,— Serving others,

CHORUS.

hope can brighten Darken'd homes below! Lighten burdens! help your broth-
manner tender To a friend in need!   [ers!
ray of gladness, By a word or gift.
lay up treasure, In the home a-bove.

This is Christ's command; Lighten burdens borne by others, With a ready hand!

Copyright, 1899, by J. Howard Entwisle.

150. The Harbor Lights of Home.

Mrs. Ida M. Budd.   Chas. H. Gabriel.

1. O'er the trackless deep the sail-or sails for many a wea-ry day,
2. O'er life's sea the Christian sail or steers his bark with stead-y hand,
3. So when fair skies bend above us, as we glide the bil-lows o'er,

Long-ing for the peace-ful ha-ven and the dear ones far a-way;
Knowing that his chart and compass will di-rect him safe to land;
Or when dark'ning shadows gath-er, and the tempests rage and roar,

But he keeps his heart with courage as his good ship parts the foam,
And he finds a calm in tu-mult, and a brightness in the gloom,
We will trust that to the ha-ven of our hopes we soon shall come,

For he knows that in the distance shine the har-bor lights of home.
As his face beholds the shin-ing of the har-bor lights of home.
Guid-ed by the stead-y gleaming of the har-bor lights of home.

CHORUS.

The home lights are shining! The home lights are shining! Bright-ly
Brightly beaming

Copyright, 1894, by Chas. H. Gabriel. John J. Hood, owner.

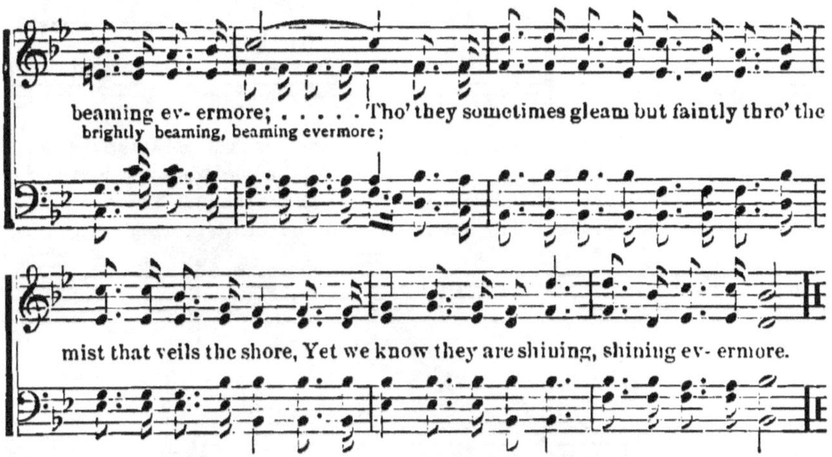

The Harbor Lights, etc.—CONCLUDED. 151

beaming ev-ermore; . . . . . Tho' they sometimes gleam but faintly thro' the
brightly beaming, beaming evermore;

mist that veils the shore, Yet we know they are shining, shining ev-ermore.

A Feast of Love To-day.

FANNY J. CROSBY. JNO. R. SWENEY.

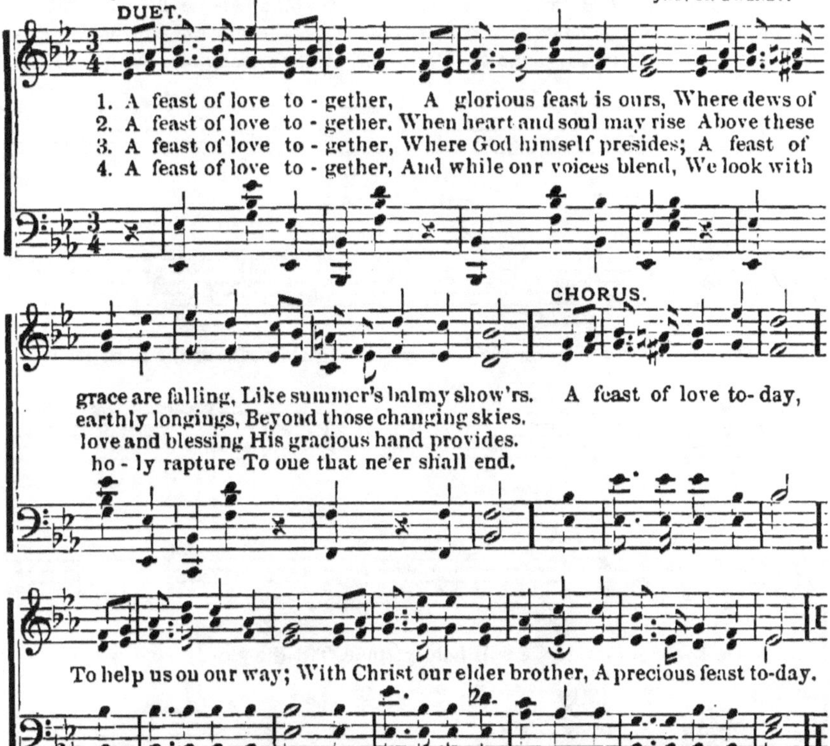

DUET.

1. A feast of love to-gether, A glorious feast is ours, Where dews of
2. A feast of love to-gether, When heart and soul may rise Above these
3. A feast of love to-gether, Where God himself presides; A feast of
4. A feast of love to-gether, And while our voices blend, We look with

CHORUS.

grace are falling, Like summer's balmy show'rs. A feast of love to-day,
earthly longings, Beyond those changing skies.
love and blessing His gracious hand provides.
ho-ly rapture To one that ne'er shall end.

To help us on our way; With Christ our elder brother, A precious feast to-day.

Copyright, 1893, by Jno. R. Sweney.

The Words of Jesus.

157

E. A. Barnes.
Jno. R. Sweney.

1. Hear the words of Jesus,— As you oft-en may, And their loving message
2. Take the words of Jesus, Hide them in your heart, And in joy or sor-row
3. Speak the words of Jesus, And their message give, That the lost and err-ing
4. Sing the words of Jesus, Sing them far and near, That the world around us

Do not put a-way; Grace that is redeem-ing In the words appear,
Let them not depart; Take the words and keep them With a spir-it true,
May return and live; Speak them to the wea-ry, As you see the need,
May the gospel hear; There is nothing sweeter, As we pass a-long,

If you will re-ceive them E-ven as you hear.
That the hope of heav-en May abide with you.
For in time of troub-le They are sweet indeed.
Than the words of Je-sus Blended in-to song.

CHORUS.

Words of Je-sus, sweet and ho-ly, Never will they pass away, Never will they pass away; Precious words of Jesus, giving life to all, Never will they pass a-way.

Copyright, 1899, by Jno. R. Sweney.

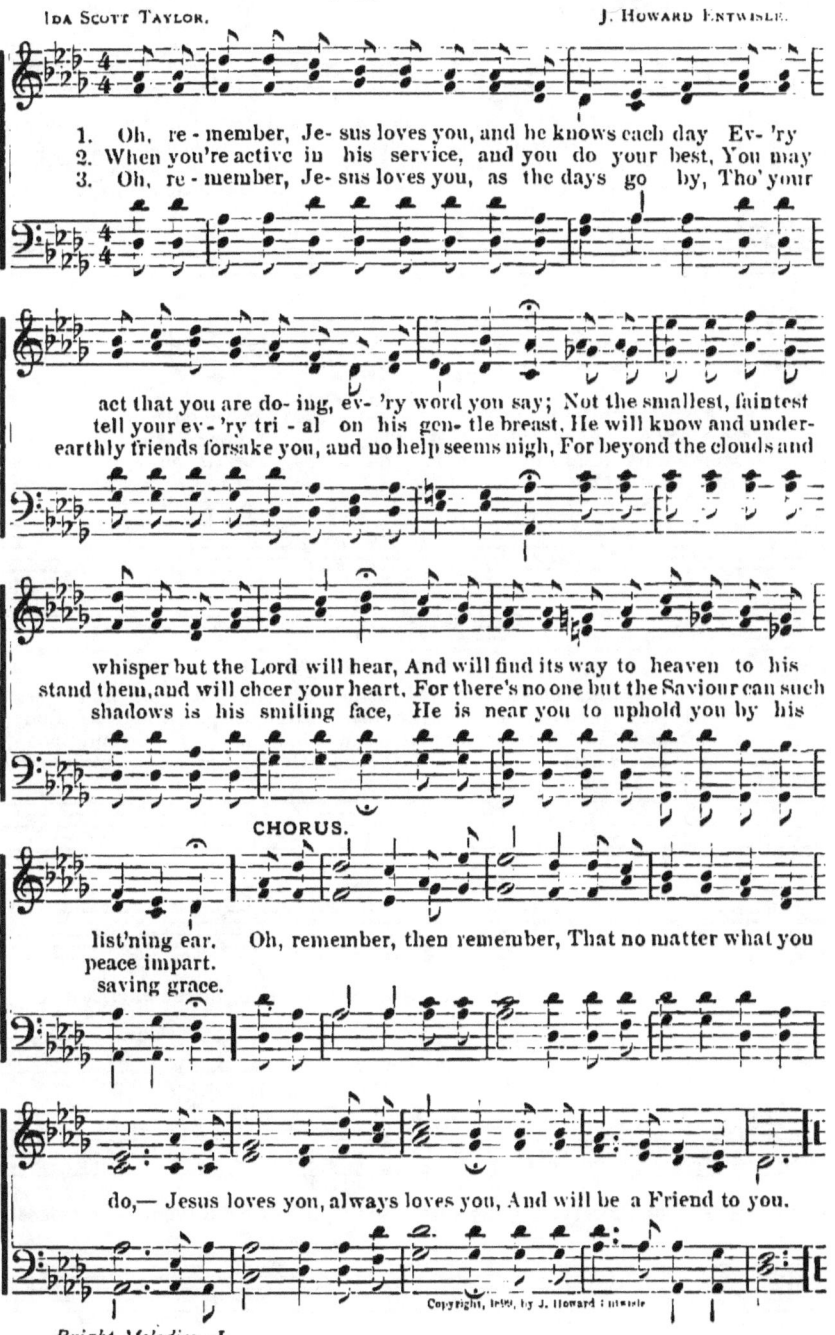

Resting By the Way.—CONCLUDED.

In communion blest and sweet, Oh, what blessed times of resting by the way.

Love Divine.

CHARLES WESLEY.   Tune, LOVE DIVINE. 8, 7, d.

1. Love di-vine, all love ex-celling, Joy of heav'n to earth come down!
Fix in us thy hum-ble dwelling! All thy faithful mer-cies crown.
D.S.—Vis-it us with thy sal-va-tion; En-ter ev-'ry trembling heart.
Je-sus, thou art all com-passion, Pure, unbounded love thou art;

2 Breathe, oh, breathe thy loving Spirit
  Into every troubled breast!
Let us all in thee inherit,
  Let us find that second rest.
Take away our bent to sinning;
  Alpha and Omega be;
End of faith, as its beginning,
  Set our hearts at liberty.

3 Come, almighty to deliver,
  Let us all thy life receive;
Suddenly return, and never,
  Never more thy temples leave,

Thee we would be always blessing,
  Serve thee as thy hosts above,
Pray, and praise thee without ceasing,
  Glory in thy perfect love.

4 Finish then thy new creation;
  Pure and spotless let us be;
Let us see thy great salvation,
  Perfectly restored in thee:
Changed from glory into glory,
  Till in heaven we take our place,
Till we cast our crowns before thee,
  Lost in wonder, love, and praise.

The New Song.—CONCLUDED.

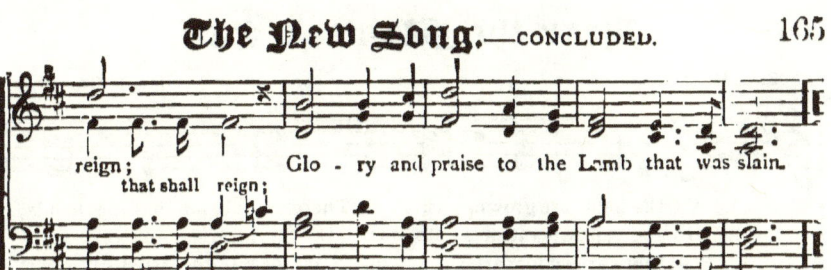

reign;
that shall reign;   Glo - ry and praise to the Lamb that was slain.

3 Can my lips be mute, or my heart be sad,
 When the gracious Master hath made me
   glad?
 When he points where the many mansions [be,
 And sweetly says, 'There is one for thee'?

4 I shall catch the gleam of its jasper wall
 When I come to the gloom of the evenfall,
 For I know that the shadows, dreary and
   dim,
 Have a path of light that will lead to him.

From "Gems of Praise," by per.

Fill Me Now.

Rev. E. H. STOKES, D.D.   JNO. R. SWENEY.

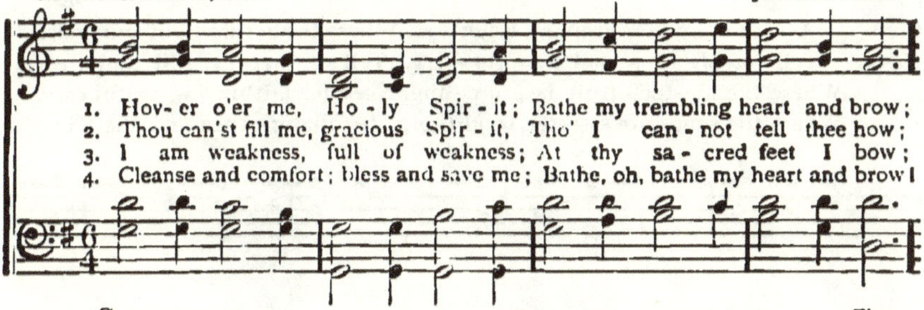

1. Hov - er o'er me, Ho - ly Spir - it; Bathe my trembling heart and brow;
2. Thou can'st fill me, gracious Spir - it, Tho' I can - not tell thee how;
3. I am weakness, full of weakness, At thy sa - cred feet I bow;
4. Cleanse and comfort; bless and save me; Bathe, oh, bathe my heart and brow!

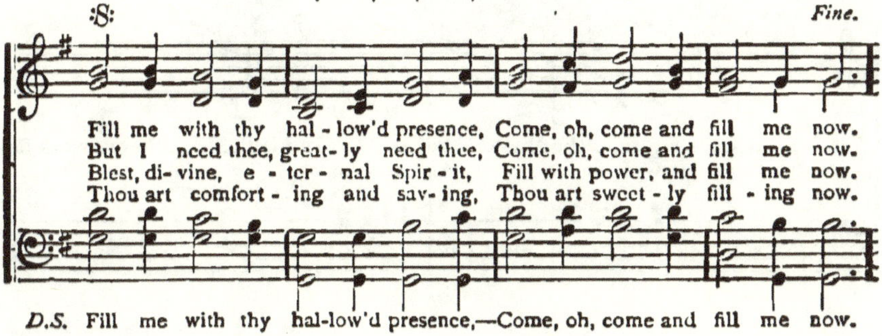

Fine.

Fill me with thy hal - low'd presence, Come, oh, come and fill me now.
But I need thee, great - ly need thee, Come, oh, come and fill me now.
Blest, di - vine, e - ter - nal Spir - it, Fill with power, and fill me now.
Thou art comfort - ing and sav - ing, Thou art sweet - ly fill - ing now.

D.S. Fill me with thy hal-low'd presence,—Come, oh, come and fill me now.

CHORUS.   *D.S.*

Fill me now, fill me now, Je - sus, come, and fill me now;

COPYRIGHT, 1879, by JOHN J. HOOD.

168. The Beautiful Land.

Fanny J. Crosby. Jno. R. Sweney.

1. We have heard of a land on whose blue, ether skies Not a cloud for a moment can stay, And it needs not the sun in his splen-dor to rise, For the Lord is the light of its day; We have heard of that land, and its glo-ry we seek, Where the faith-ful with

2. We have talked of that land when our jour-ney was long, And our hearts overburdened with care, We have talked of the blest at the riv-er of song, And how oft we have sighed to be there; And our faith has gone up, like a bird on the wing, To that land on e-

3. We are near-ing that land, we are near-ing the gate To the cit-y of jas-per and gold, Where the Saviour to welcome his children doth wait, And will gath-er them in-to the fold; To the fold of his love, in the mansions a-bove, Where for-ev-er with

Copyright, 1890, by Jno. R. Sweney.

Sow Kind Deeds.

Myron W. Morse.
J. Howard Entwisle.

1. Sow kind deeds in youth's fair morning, Sow kind deeds where'er you go, And believe that at the harvest You shall reap just as you sow; Ev-'ry kindness freely given, God in love takes note of all, For without his loving mercy, E'en the sparrow cannot fall.

2. Sow bright smiles amid life's sorrows, Sow bright smiles where'er you go, For the sweetness you may scatter May set some sad heart aglow; Then perchance to some in darkness Sunshine may illume the way, Sow bright smiles the livelong day.

3. Sow kind deeds in early morning, Sow kind deeds till close of day, You may meet a heart discourag'd, You may brighten life's rough way; Sow kind deeds and then remember, Guardian angels will record Ev-'ry worthy deed or action, Ev'ry cheering smile or word.

CHORUS.

Sow kind deeds in the morning, Sow kind deeds at noontide, [early morning, sunny noontide,] You may brighten life's weary way, Then sow kind deeds all the day.

Copyright, 1898, by John J. Hood.

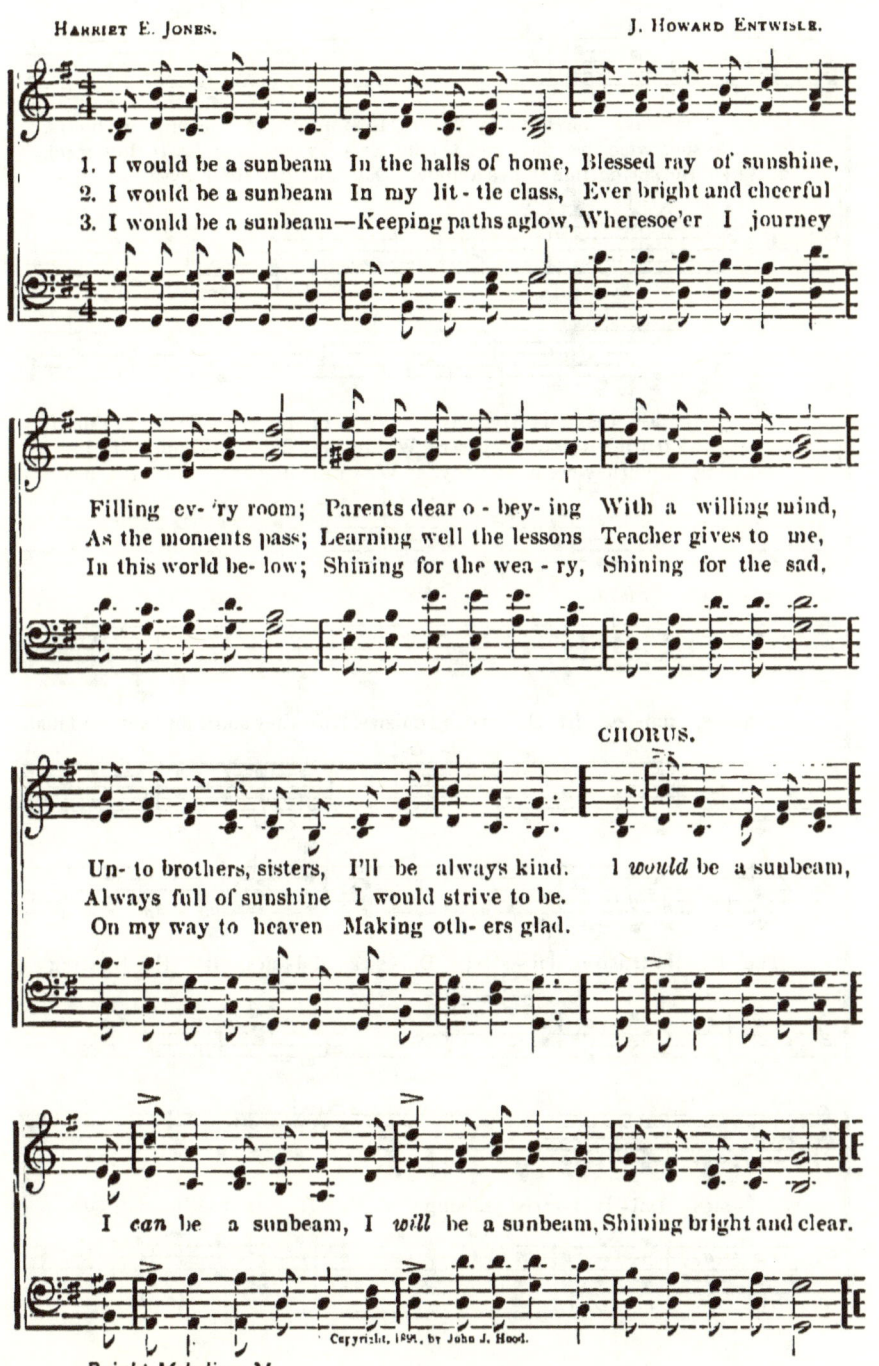

God will Remember.

IDA SCOTT TAYLOR.   J. HOWARD ENTWISLE.

1. Hum, little bee, in the nodding clover, Swing, little bird, in the tree-top tall,
2. Bloom, little flow'r, in the valley vernal, Flow, little brook, to the deep wide sea.
3. Trust, little heart, for the Lord is near you, Sing, little voice, make his glories [known;

God in the heavens is watching over, He will remember his creatures all.
Held in the hand of the Great Eternal, Kept by the love that is full and free.
Speak, little tongue, for the King will hear you, He will remember and guard his own.

CHORUS.

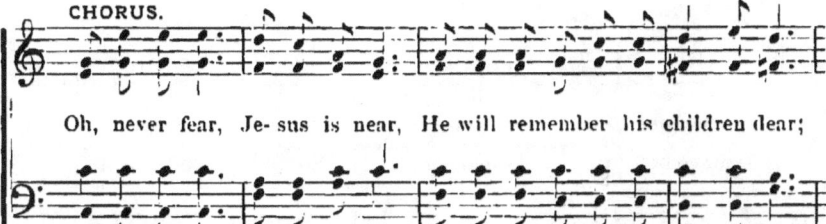

Oh, never fear, Je-sus is near, He will remember his children dear;

Oh, never fear, Je-sus is near, He will remember his children dear.

Copyright, 1898, by John J. Hood.

180 The Coming of the King.

E. E. Hewitt. Jno. R. Sweney.

1. Rejoice, rejoice, the wilderness shall bloom, New beams the sky illume, New beams the sky illume, And song shall banish winter's gloom, Jesus comes! The long, long years are past, Our King has come at last, And hearts with joy are beating fast, For Jesus comes. Stars are burning brightly, Flocks in slumber lie, Breathes the wind-harp light-ly, Na-ture's lul-la-by,

2. Rejoice, rejoice, for Sharon's royal Rose Its beauties will disclose, Its beauties will disclose; The east with rosy splendor glows, Jesus comes! O sing his reign of love, While mercy smiles above, Peace folds her wings like gentle dove, For Jesus comes. In ... the manger low-ly, Sleeps the wondrous Child, Oh, ... how fair and ho-ly! Oh, ... how pure and mild!

Rejoice, rejoice,
Golden stars brightly burn, Flocks at rest, sleeping lie,
Christ is born, Christ is born, Sleeps the Child, wondrous child,
Lightly breathes, lightly breathes Lul-la-by, lul-la-by,
Fairest Child, ho-ly Child, Pure and mild, pure and mild,

Copyright, 1887, by John J. Hood.

There is Joy, etc.—CONCLUDED.

Joy, joy, joy o-ver all the earth, There is joy at Christmas time.

The Night has Passed Away.

E. A. BARNES. JNO. R. SWENEY.

1. The night has passed away, Je-sus is born! We hail the golden day,
2. The love of God appears, Je-sus is born! To bless this vale of tears,
3. Let all look up and sing, Je-sus is born! Let earth with praises ring,

Je-sus is born! We have the gift of love From shining courts above,
Je-sus is born! Above his lowly bed The light of God is shed,
Je-sus is born! Let tokens sweet abound, Let hope and peace be found,

1. We have the gift of love From shin - ing courts above,

And there is heard the joyful word, Je-sus is born! Je-sus is born!
And we repeat the message sweet, Je-sus is born! Je-sus is born!
Let all to-day rejoice and say, Je-sus is born! Je-sus is born!

Copyright, 1898, by Jno. R. Sweney.

Precious Gifts of Love.—CONCLUDED. 185

Free to all, free to all! our full sal-vation, Free to all! (Free to all!)

The Bells are Calling.

FANNY J. CROSBY.   JNO. R. SWENEY.

1. Come a-way, the bells are call-ing, Mer-ry bells of Christmas time;
2. Come a-way, they still are call-ing, While, to crown our fes-tal scene,
3. Come a-way, our faith is call-ing, And we look with lov-ing eyes
4. Come a-way, our souls are call-ing, While the bells responsive ring;

Youthful hearts again are bounding While we catch their tuneful chime.
Bus-y fingers now are twin-ing Wreaths of hol-ly bright and green.
On a low-ly manger cra-dle Where the in-fant Saviour lies.
Hal-le-lu-jah in the high-est To the Lord's a-nointed King!

CHORUS.

Merry, merry bells, merry, merry bells, Listen to their carol and the joy it tells;
Merry, merry Christmas bells, merry, merry Christmas bells,

Ringing far and near, ringing sweet and clear, O the blessed music of the old-time
Ringing, ringing far and near, ringing, ringing sweet and clear,   [bells.

Copyright, 1889, by Jno. R. Sweney.

Roses Everywhere.

IDA SCOTT TAYLOR.   J. HOWARD ENTWISLE.

DUET.

1. Ro-ses, ro-ses, sum-mer ro-ses, What de-lights the June dis-closes, What a song the sea-son sings With the love-ly flow'rs she brings! (she brings!)
2. Ro-ses, ro-ses, vel-vet ro-ses, That the Win-ter-King op-poses, How they cheer the sons of men, When the spring-time comes a-gain. (again.)
3. Ro-ses, ro-ses, love-ly ro-ses, Mother Earth in bliss re-poses, Covered o-ver in her rest With the flow'rs we love the best. (the best.)

CHORUS.

Earth is like a garden fair, Roses blooming ev-'rywhere; Nodding, nodding, brightly, gai-ly, Budding, blooming, hourly, dai-ly, Red and yellow, pink and white, Sending sweetness

Copyright, 1898, by John J. Hood.

Roses Everywhere.—CONCLUDED.

left and right; What a perfume fills the air, Ro- ses, ro- ses ev'rywhere!

Sweet Sabbath Bells.

F. M. D.   "Let us go into the house of the Lord."—Ps. cxxii : 1.   FRANK M. DAVIS.

1. Sweet the music of the Sabbath bells, Stealing on the qui - et air,
2. Sweet the music of the Sabbath bells, As they to the world proclaim,
3. Sweet the music of the Sabbath bells; Let it ech - o earth around,

Floating o'er the world in tuneful notes, Calling to the house of pray'r.
"Who- so- ev - er will, may find sweet rest Thro' the blessed Saviour's name."
Till the nations now in darkness hear And shall know the gospel sound.

CHORUS.

Chime on, chime on, sweet Sabbath bells, chime on, chime on,
Chime on, chime on, chime on, chime on,

Chime on, chime on, sweet Sabbath bells, chime on.
Chime on, chime on, chime on, chime on,

From "Notes of Praise," By per. of John J. Hood.

Do the Best You Can.

E. E. Rexford.
Jno. R. Bryant.

1. If clouds blot out the sunshine A-long the path you tread, Don't grieve in hopeless fashion, And sigh for brightness fled; Beyond the cloud the sunlight Shines in God's changeless plan. Trust that the way will brighten, And do the best you can.

2. A-way with vain repin-ing! Sing songs of hope and cheer, Till many a wea-ry comrade Grows strong of heart to hear; He who sings o-ver trouble, With faith in God a-bove, Sees thro' earth's clouds the sunshine Of God's e-ter-nal love.

3. So in the time of trouble Let not your courage fail. The clouds must sometime van-ish, The sun at last pre-vail; Trust we th' e-ter-nal goodness, The all-wise Father's plan, And, brave with hope and courage, Do just the best you can.

D.S.—Let not your courage fal-ter, Keep faith in God and man, And all a-long life's pathway Do just the best you can.

CHORUS.

Then do your best, Yes, do the best you can; Then do your best, Yes, do the best you can;
Then do the best you can, Then do the best you can,

Copyright, 1899, by John J. Hood.

Lend a Hand.—CONCLUDED.

Nearer, My God, to Thee!

Mrs. SARAH F. ADAMS. Rev. S. G. NEIL.

Copyright, 1896, by Jno R. Sweney.

2 Though like the wanderer,
   The sun gone down,
   Darkness be over me,
   My rest a stone,
   Yet in my dreams I'd be
   Nearer, my God, to thee,
   Nearer to thee!

3 There let the way appear,
   Steps unto heaven;
   All that thou sendest me,
   In mercy given,
   Angels to beckon me
   Nearer, my God, to thee,
   Nearer to thee!
Bright Melodies—N

4 Then, with my waking thoughts
   Bright with thy praise,
   Out of my stony griefs
   Bethel I'll raise;
   So by my woes to be
   Nearer, my God, to thee,
   Nearer to thee!

5 Or if, on joyful wing
   Cleaving the sky,
   Sun, moon, and stars forgot,
   Upward I fly,
   Still all my song shall be,
   Nearer, my God, to thee,
   Nearer to thee!

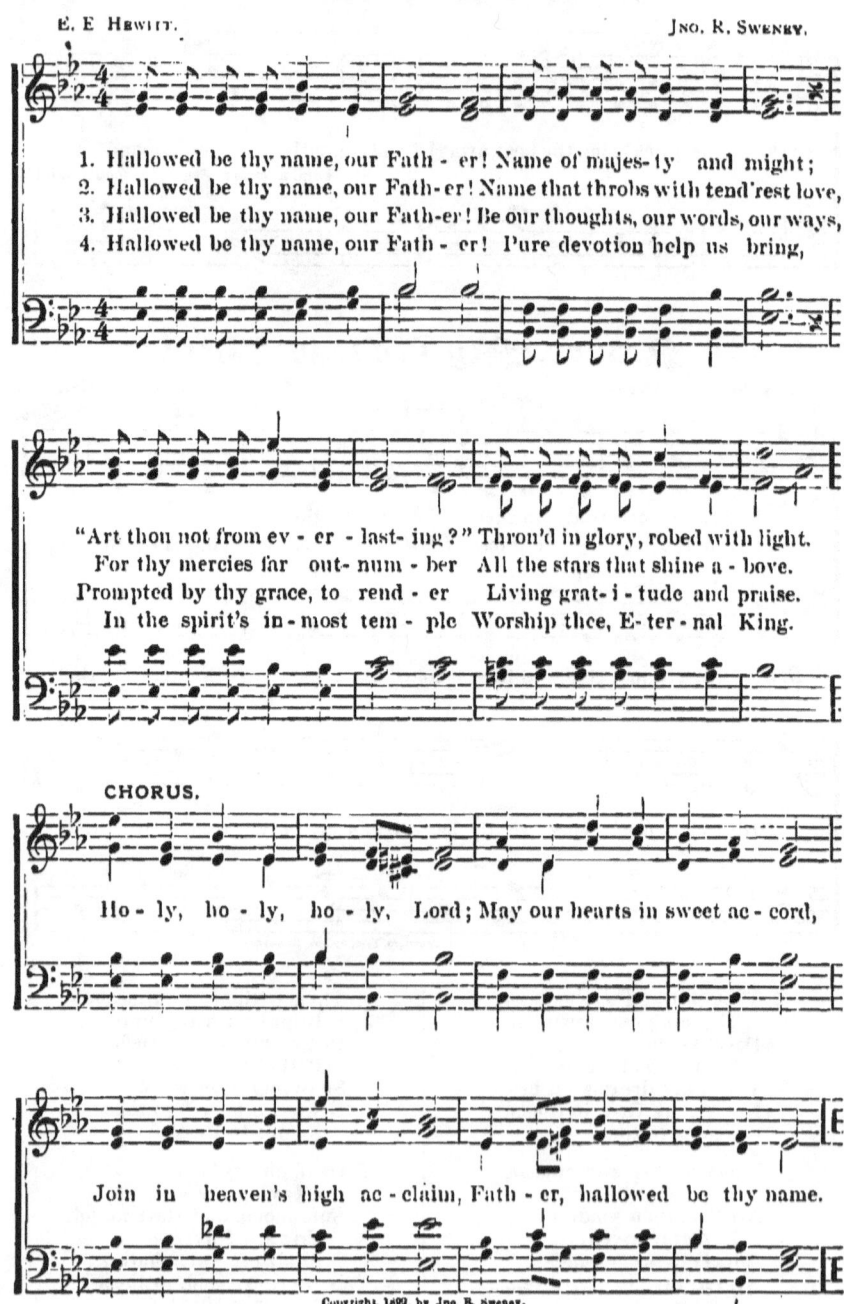

4 On to glory I am marching,
　　While a Friend is by my side;
　I shall never fall nor falter
　　If he leads, my faithful Guide.

5 On to glory, nearer, nearer,
　　Nearer to that angel-throng;
　I can almost hear the music
　　In the land of endless song.

4 The way to heav'n we may pursue,
  Step by step, step by step;
  And keep the cross and crown in view,
  Walking step by step.

5 The life divine we can attain,
  Step by step, step by step;
  And rise at last with him to reign,
  Walking step by step.

I will Say "Yes" to Jesus.—CONCLUDED. 201

With outstretch'd hands my Saviour stands, And beckons the wand'rer to come;
the wand'rer to come;

Without de-lay I'll now o-bey, And he will welcome me home. . . .
will welcome me home.

Come to Me.

Mrs. J. C. Yule. E. O. Excell.

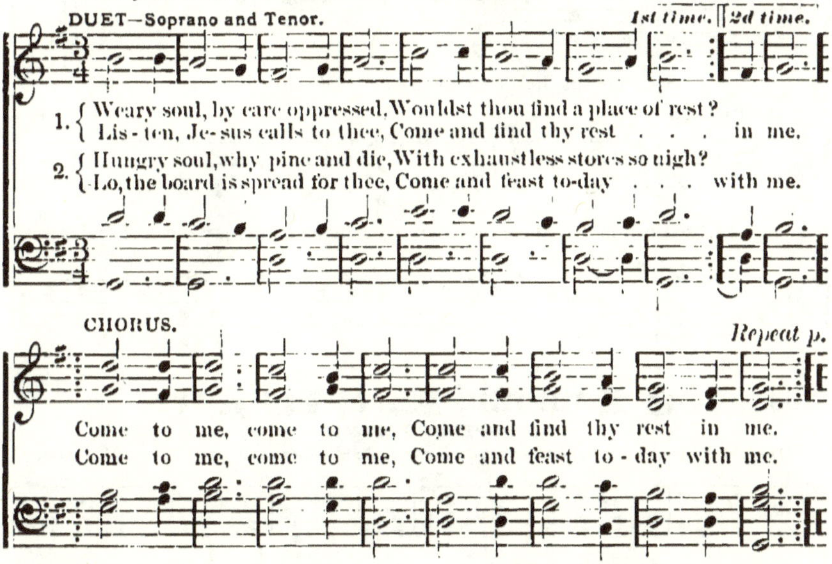

DUET—Soprano and Tenor. *1st time.* ‖ *2d time.*

1. { Weary soul, by care oppressed, Wouldst thou find a place of rest?
     Lis-ten, Je-sus calls to thee, Come and find thy rest . . . in me.
2. { Hungry soul, why pine and die, With exhaustless stores so nigh?
     Lo, the board is spread for thee, Come and feast to-day . . . with me.

CHORUS. *Repeat p.*

Come to me, come to me, Come and find thy rest in me.
Come to me, come to me, Come and feast to-day with me.

3 Thirsty soul, earth's sweetest rill
   Mocks thee with its promise still;
   Hark, the Saviour calls to thee,
   Here is water, come to me.

CHO.—Come to me, come to me,
     Here is water, come to me.

4 Heavenly bread and heavenly wine,
   Living waters,—all are mine,
   Mine they are and thine may be;
   Weary wand'rer, come to me.

CHO.—Come to me, come to me,
     Weary wand'rer, come to me.

Copyright, 1881, by John J. Hood.

202. Blessed Union.

FANNY J. CROSBY.   JNO. R. SWENEY.

1. Blessed union, sweet communion, With the Father and the Son;
2. With a perfect trust abiding, In the life eternal word,
3. Blessed union, sweet communion, On the wings of faith we rise;
4. Blessed union, sweet communion, Higher yet our hopes ascend;

Thro' the triumph, wondrous triumph, That redeeming grace has won.
Who shall sever us forever From the love of Christ the Lord?
Now our title reading clearly, To a mansion in the skies.
Glory, glory, all is glory! Growing brighter to the end.

D.S.—Jesus, heirs together Of the glory yet to be.

CHORUS.   *D.S.*

Blessed union, sweet communion, Oh, the constant joy we see! Heirs with

Copyright, 1899, by Jno. R. Sweney.

203. O Saviour, Meet Us Here.
OPENING HYMN.

HARRIET E. JONES.   "None other but the house of God."—Gen. xxiii: 17.   FRANK M. DAVIS.

1. Within thy courts, O Lord, We meet this sacred day, To render praise and
2. May this, our op'ning hymn Be pleasant to our King; May faith grow bright that
3. And when we kneel in pray'r, May ev'ry heart be free From worldly tho'ts and

From "Notes of Praise." By per. of John J. Hood.

205. Some Sweet Day.

HARRIET E. JONES.   FRANK M. DAVIS.

1. We shall cross the rolling tide, Some sweet day, yes, some sweet day; We shall
2. We shall tread the streets of gold, Some sweet day, yes, some sweet day; Heaven's
3. Yes, we'll reach the home of God, Some sweet day, yes, some sweet day; Thro' the

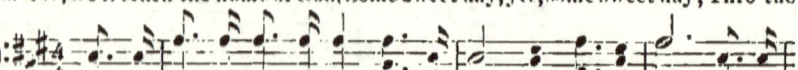

Cho. We shall cross the rolling tide, Some sweet day, yes, some sweet day; We shall

gain the golden side, Some sweet day, yes, some sweet day; Near the crystal waters
splendor shall behold, Some sweet day, yes, some sweet day; We shall find the mansions
precious, precious blood, Some sweet day, yes, some sweet day; Never there to sigh a-

gain the golden side, Some sweet day, yes, some sweet day.

roam, In the saint's eternal home, Where the shadows never come; Some sweet day.
fair, Jesus promis'd to prepare, That are waiting over there; Some sweet day.
gain, Never tho't of grief or pain, Evermore with Christ to reign; Some sweet day.

From "Notes of Praise." By per. of John J. Hood.

206. Bright Little Sunbeams.

MAY JESS FLEMING.   RAN. C. STOREY.

DUET.

1. We are Je- sus' lit- tle sunbeams, Shining e'er so bright; We will drive a-
2. We are Je- sus' lit- tle sunbeams, Shining all we can; We would light some
3. We are Je- sus' lit- tle sunbeams, O- vercoming wrong; We are telling

Copyright, 1892, by John J. Hood.

Bright Little Sunbeams.—CONCLUDED.

CHORUS.

way all sadness, With our cheerful light. We are bright little sunbeams,
lone- ly pathway, 'Tis our settled plan.
of his goodness In a cheerful song.

Shining on the way; We are bright little sunbeams, Shining all the day.

---

207   **Come, O Come.**

FANNY J. CROSBY.   "A fountain is opened for sin."—Zech. xiii: 1.   FRANK M. DAVIS.

1. Je-sus has open'd up a fountain, Where weary, sin-sick souls may go;
2. Many have wash'd in these pure waters, Wash'd all their stains as white as snow;
3. They who are pure in heart are blessed, They heaven's joys alone shall know;

Hear him in tender accents say-ing, "Come where the healing waters flow."
Oh, may the millions hear the message, "Come where the healing waters flow."
Who then would fail to heed the message, "Come where the healing waters flow?"

D. S.—"Come where the healing waters flow."

CHORUS.   *D. S.*

Come, O come! Come, O come! Hear him in tender accents saying,
Come, O come! come, O come! Come, O come! come, O come!

From "Notes of Praise." By per. of John J. Hood.

208. My Jesus, as Thou wilt.

BENJAMIN SCHMOLKA. Tr. by Miss J. BORTHWICK.   Tune, JEWETT. 6s.

1. My Jesus, as thou wilt: O may thy will be mine; In-to thy hand of love I would my all re-sign. Thro' sor-row or thro' joy, Conduct me as thine own, And help me still to say, "My Lord, thy will be done."
2. My Jesus, as thou wilt: Tho' seen thro' many-a tear, Let not my star of hope Grow dim or dis-ap-pear. Since thou on earth hast wept And sorrowed oft alone, If I must weep with thee, My Lord, thy will be done.
3. My Jesus, as thou wilt: All shall be well for me; Each changing fu-ture scene I glad-ly trust with thee. Straight to my home a-bove, I trav-el calmly on, And sing in life or death, "My Lord, thy will be done."

209. Holy, holy, holy.

REGINALD HEBER.   Tune, NICEA. 11, 12, 10.

1. Ho-ly, ho-ly, ho-ly, Lord God Almight-y! Ear-ly in the
2. Ho-ly, ho-ly, ho-ly! all the saints adore thee, Casting down their
3. Ho-ly, ho-ly, ho-ly! tho' the darkness hide thee, Tho' the eye of
4. Ho-ly, ho-ly, ho-ly,. Lord God Almight-y! All thy works shall

Holy, holy, holy.—CONCLUDED.

morn - ing our song shall rise to thee; Holy, holy, holy,
gold-en crowns around the glas-sy sea; Cher-u-bim and seraphim
sin-ful man thy glo-ry may not see; On-ly thou art ho-ly!
praise thy name, in earth, and sky, and sea; Holy, holy, holy,

mer-ci-ful and might-y, God in Three Persons, blessed Trin-i-ty!
falling down before thee, Which wert and art, and evermore shalt be.
there is none be-side thee, Per-fect in power, in love, and pur-i-ty.
mer-ci-ful and might-y, God in Three Persons, blessed Trin-i-ty!

210. Rock of Ages.
Tune, TOPLADY. 7.

1. Rock of a - ges, cleft for me, Let me hide myself in thee;
D. C.—Be of sin the double cure,—Cleanse me from its guilt and pow'r.

Let the wa-ter and the blood From thy wounded side which flowed,

2 Not the labor of my hands,
Can fulfil the law's demands;
Could my zeal no respite know,
Could my tears forever flow,
All for sin could not atone,—
Thou must save, and thou alone.

3 Nothing in my hand I bring;
Simply to thy cross I cling;
Naked, come to thee for dress,

Helpless, look to thee for grace,—
Vile, I to the fountain fly,
Wash me, Saviour, or I die.

4 While I draw this fleeting breath,
When my heart-strings break in death,
When I soar to worlds unknown,
See thee on thy judgement-throne,—
Rock of ages, cleft for me,
Let me hide myself in thee.

Is my Name written There?

M. A. K.
Frank M. Davis. By per.

1. Lord, I care not for rich-es, Neither sil-ver nor gold; I would make sure of heaven, I would en-ter the fold. In the book of thy kingdom, With its pa-ges so fair, Tell me, Je-sus, my Sav-iour, Is my name written there?

2. Lord, my sins they are ma-ny, Like the sands of the sea, But thy blood, Oh, my Sa-viour! Is suf-fi-cient for me; For thy promise is written, In bright let-ters that glow, "Though your sins be as scarlet, I will make them like snow."

3. Oh! that beau-ti-ful cit-y, With its mansions of light, With its glo-ri-fied be-ings, In pure garments of white; Where no e-vil thing cometh, To de-spoil what is fair; Where the angels are watching,—Is my name written there?

Chorus.

Is my name writ-ten there, On the page white and fair? In the book of thy king-dom, Is my name writ-ten there?

4 Crowns and thrones may perish,
  Kingdoms rise and wane,
But the Church of Jesus
  Constant will remain;
Gates of hell can never
  'Gainst that Church prevail;
We have Christ's own promise,
  And that cannot fail.

5 Onward, then, ye people!
  Join our happy throng,
Blend with ours your voices
  In the triumph-song;
Glory, laud, and honor
  Unto Christ the King,
This through countless ages
  Men and angels sing.

The Mind of Jesus.

E. E. Hewitt.
Jno. R. Sweney.

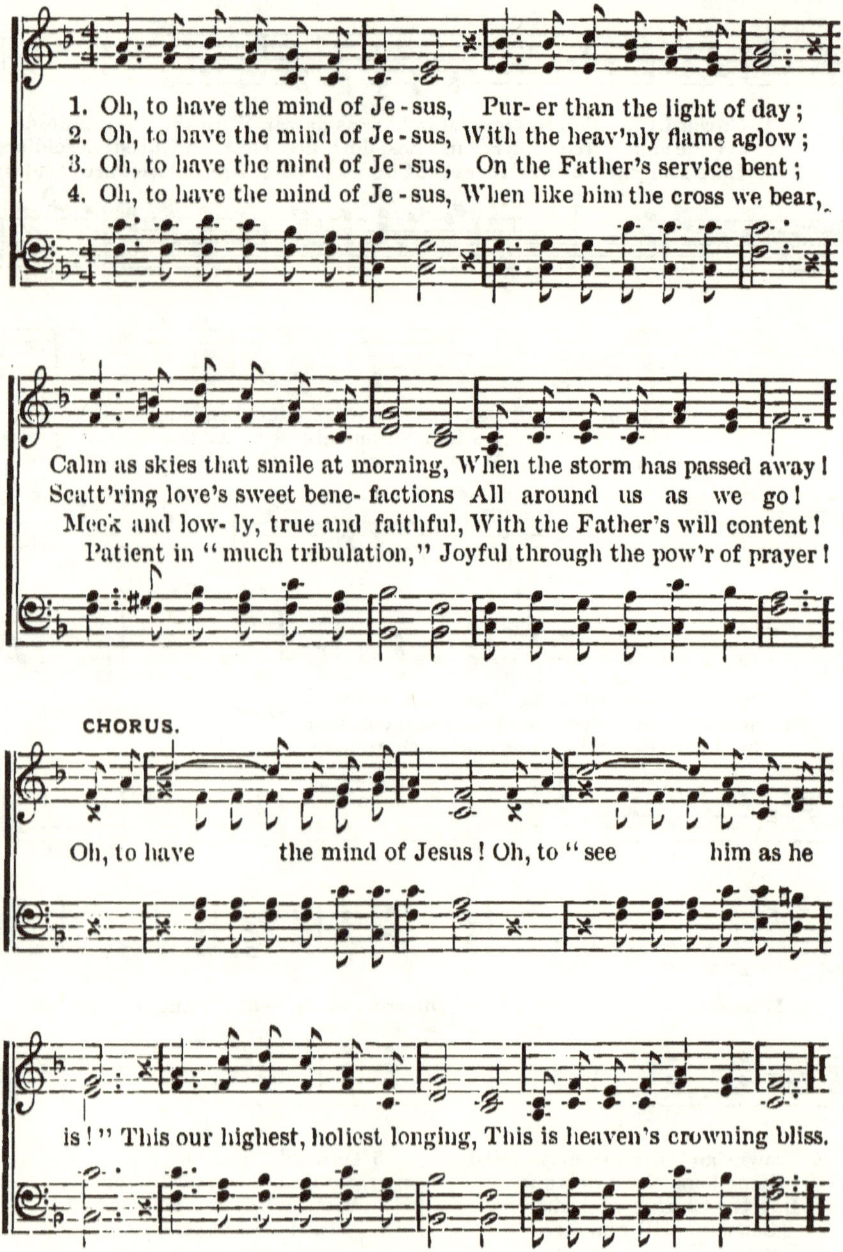

1. Oh, to have the mind of Jesus, Purer than the light of day;
2. Oh, to have the mind of Jesus, With the heav'nly flame aglow;
3. Oh, to have the mind of Jesus, On the Father's service bent;
4. Oh, to have the mind of Jesus, When like him the cross we bear,

Calm as skies that smile at morning, When the storm has passed away!
Scatt'ring love's sweet bene- factions All around us as we go!
Meek and low- ly, true and faithful, With the Father's will content!
Patient in "much tribulation," Joyful through the pow'r of prayer!

CHORUS.

Oh, to have the mind of Jesus! Oh, to "see him as he is!" This our highest, holiest longing, This is heaven's crowning bliss.

Copyright, 1890, by Jno. R. Sweney.

The Firm Foundation.

GEORGE KEITH.   Tune, PORTUGUESE HYMN.

1. How firm a foundation, ye saints of the Lord, Is laid for your faith in his ex-cel-lent word ! What more can he say, than to you he hath said, To you, who for re-fuge to Je-sus have fled? To you, who for re-fuge to Je-sus have fled?

2. "Fear not, I am with thee, O be not dismayed, For I am thy God, I will still give thee aid; I'll strengthen thee, help thee, and cause thee to stand, Up-held by my gracious, om-ni-po-tent hand, Up-held by my gracious, om-ni-po-tent hand.

3. "When thro' the deep waters I call thee to go, The riv-ers of sor-row shall not o-ver-flow; For I will be with thee thy tri-als to bless, And sanc-ti-fy to thee thy deepest dis-tress, And sanc-ti-fy to thee thy deep-est dis-tress.

4. "When thro' fie-ry tri-als thy path-way shall lie, My grace all suf-fi-cient, shall be thy sup-ply, The flame shall not hurt thee; I on-ly de-sign Thy dross to consume, and thy gold to re-fine, Thy dross to consume, and thy gold to re-fine.

5 "E'en down to old age all my people shall prove
My sovereign, eternal, unchangeable [love;
And when hoary hairs shall their temples adorn,
Like lambs they shall still in my bosom [be borne.

6 "The soul that on Jesus hath leaned for repose,
I will not, I will not desert to his foes;
That soul, though all hell should endeavor to shake,
I'll never, no never, no never forsake!"

216. I am Coming to the Cross.

Rev. Wm. McDonald. — John vi. 37. — Wm. G. Fischer. By per.

1. I am com-ing to the cross; I am poor, and weak, and blind;
2. Long my heart has sighed for thee, Long has e-vil dwelt within;
3. Here I give my all to thee, Friends, and time, and earthly store;

Cho.—I am trust-ing, Lord, in thee, Blest Lamb of Cal-va-ry;

I am count-ing all but dross, I shall full sal-va-tion find.
Je-sus sweet-ly speaks to me.— "I will cleanse you from all sin."
Soul and bo-dy thine to be,—Whol-ly thine for ev-er-more.

Humbly at thy cross I bow, Save me, Je-sus, save me now.

4 In thy promises I trust,
 Now I feel the blood applied:
 I am prostrate in the dust,
 I with Christ am crucified.

5 Jesus comes! he fills my soul!
 Perfected in him I am;
 I am every whit made whole:
 Glory, glory to the Lamb.

217. Happy Day.

P. Doddridge. — English Melody.

1. O happy day, that fixed my choice On thee, my Saviour and my God!
 Well may this glowing heart rejoice, And tell its raptures all abroad.
 Happy day, happy day, When Jesus washed my sins away!
 He taught me how to watch and pray, And live rejoicing ev'ry day.

2 O happy bond, that seals my vows
 To him who merits all my love!
 Let cheerful anthems fill his house,
 While to that sacred shrine I move.

3 'Tis done! the great transaction's done!
 I am my Lord's, and he is mine:
 He drew me, and I followed on,
 Charmed to confess that voice divine.

4 Now rest, my long-divided heart;
 Fixed on this blissful center, rest;
 Nor ever from thy Lord depart;
 With him of every good possessed.

5 High heav'n that heard the solemn vow,
 That vow renewed shall daily hear,
 Till in life's latest hour I bow,
 And bless in death a bond so dear.

218 When all Thy Mercies.

JOSEPH ADDISON.   Tune, MANOAH. C.M.

1. When all thy mer-cies, O my God, My ris-ing soul sur-veys,
2. Through hidden dangers, toils, and deaths, It gently cleared my way;

Transport-ed with the view, I'm lost In won-der, love, and praise.
And through the pleasing snares of vice, More to be feared than they.

3 Through every period of my life
   Thy goodness I'll pursue;
And after death, in distant worlds,
   The pleasing theme renew.

4 Through all eternity to thee
   A grateful song I'll raise;
But oh, eternity's too short
   To utter all thy praise.

219 How Sweet the Name.

JOHN NEWTON.   Tune, DOWNS. C.M.

1. How sweet the name of Je-sus sounds In a be-liev-er's ear!
It soothes his sor-rows, heals his wounds, And drives away his fear.

2 It makes the wounded spirit whole,
   And calms the troubled breast;
'Tis manna to the hungry soul,
   And to the weary, rest.

3 Dear name! the rock on which I build,
   My shield and hiding-place;
My never-failing treasure, filled
   With boundless stores of grace!

4 Jesus, my Shepherd, Saviour, Friend,
   My Prophet, Priest, and King,
My Lord, my Life, my Way, my End,
   Accept the praise I bring!

5 I would thy boundless love proclaim
   With every fleeting breath;
So shall the music of thy name
   Refresh my soul in death.

220. Jesus, the Name.

C. Wesley. Tune, CORONATION. C. M.

1. Je-sus! the name high o-ver all, In hell, or earth, or sky;
An-gels and men be-fore it fall, And dev-ils fear and fly.

2. Je-sus! the name to sin-ners dear, The name to sin-ners given;
It scat-ters all their guilt-y fear; It turns their hell to heaven.

3 Jesus the prisoner's fetters breaks,
   And bruises Satan's head;
Power into strengthless souls he speaks,
   And life into the dead.

4 O that the world might taste and see
   The riches of his grace!
The arms of love that compass me
   Would all mankind embrace.

5 His only righteousness I show
   His saving truth proclaim:
'Tis all my business here below,
   To cry, "Behold the Lamb!"

6 Happy, if with my latest breath
   I may but gasp his name;
Preach him to all, and cry in death,
   "Behold, behold the Lamb!"

221. Crown Him Lord of All. C. M.

1 All hail the power of Jesus' name!
   Let angels prostrate fall;
Bring forth the royal diadem,
   And crown him Lord of all.

2 Crown him, ye morning stars of light,
   Who fixed this earthly ball;
Now hail the strength of Israel's might,
   And crown him Lord of all.

3 Ye chosen seed of Israel's race,
   Ye ransomed from the fall,
Hail him who saves you by his grace,
   And crown him Lord of all.

4 Sinners, whose love can ne'er forget
   The wormwood and the gall,
Go, spread your trophies at his feet,
   And crown him Lord of all.

5 Let every kindred, every tribe,
   On this terrestrial ball,
To him all majesty ascribe,
   And crown him Lord of all.

6 O that with yonder sacred throng
   We at his feet may fall!
We'll join the everlasting song,
   And crown him Lord of all.

Antioch. C. M.

222   O for a thousand tongues.

1 O FOR a thousand tongues, to sing
My great Redeemer's praise;
The glories of my God and King,
The triumphs of his grace!

2 My gracious Master and my God,
Assist me to proclaim,
To spread through all the earth abroad,
The honors of thy name.

3 Jesus! the name that charms our fears,
That bids our sorrows cease;
'Tis music in the sinner's ears,
'Tis life, and health, and peace.

4 He breaks the power of canceled sin,
He sets the prisoner free;
His blood can make the foulest clean;
His blood availed for me.

5 He speaks, and, listening to his voice,
New life the dead receive;
The mournful, broken hearts rejoice;
The humble poor believe.

6 Hear him, ye deaf; his praise, ye dumb,
Your loosened tongues employ;
Ye blind, behold your Saviour come;
And leap, ye lame, for joy.

223   Joy to the world!

1 Joy to the world! the Lord is come;
Let earth receive her King;
Let every heart prepare him room,
And heaven and nature sing.

2 Joy to the world! the Saviour reigns;
Let men their songs employ;
While fields and floods, rocks, hills and plains
Repeat the sounding joy.

3 No more let sin and sorrow grow,
Nor thorns infest the ground;
He comes to make his blessings flow
Far as the curse is found.

4 He rules the world with truth and grace,
And makes the nations prove
The glories of his righteousness,
And wonders of his love.

224   The Lord's Prayer.

Reverently.

1. Our Father who art in heaven, hallowed | be thy | name, || Thy kingdom come, thy will be done in | earth, as-it | is in | heaven.

2. Give us this day our | daily | bread, || And forgive us our trespasses, as we forgive | them that | trespass a- | gainst us.

3. And lead us not into temptation, but deliver | us from | evil; || For thine is the kingdom, and the power and the | glory for- | ever and | ever. || A- | men.

225. The Morning Light.

Samuel F. Smith. — Tune, WEBB. 7, 6.

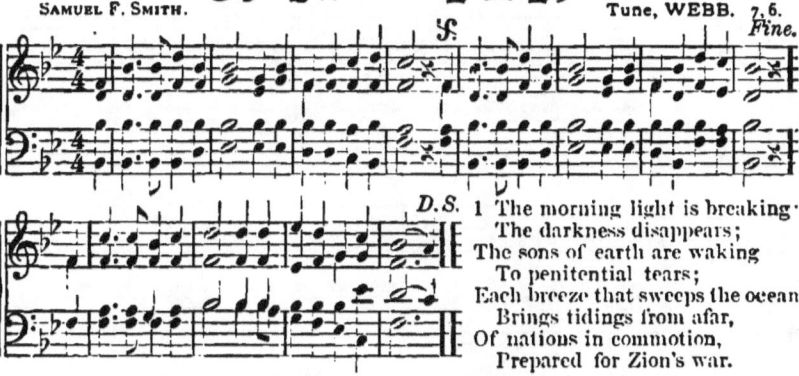

1 The morning light is breaking·
The darkness disappears;
The sons of earth are waking
To penitential tears;
Each breeze that sweeps the ocean
Brings tidings from afar,
Of nations in commotion,
Prepared for Zion's war.

2 See heathen nations bending
Before the God we love,
And thousand hearts ascending
In gratitude above;
While sinners, now confessing,
The gospel call obey,
And seek the Saviour's blessing,
A nation in a day.

3 Blest river of salvation,
Pursue thine onward way;
Flow thou to every nation,
Nor in thy richness stay:
Stay not till all the lowly
Triumphant reach their home:
Stay not till all the holy
Proclaim, "The Lord is come!"

226. Geo. Duffield, Jr. — Stand up, stand up for Jesus.
Tune above.

1 Stand up, stand up for Jesus,
Ye soldiers of the cross;
Lift high his royal banner,
It must not suffer loss;
From victory unto victory
His army shall he lead
Till every foe is vanquished
And Christ is Lord indeed.

2 Stand up, stand up for Jesus,
The trumpet call obey;
Forth to the mighty conflict,
In this his glorious day:
"Ye that are men, now serve him,"
Against unnumbered foes:
Your courage rise with danger,
And strength to strength oppose.

3 Stand up, stand up for Jesus,
Stand in his strength alone;
The arm of flesh will fail you;
Ye dare not trust your own:
Put on the gospel armor,
Each piece put on with prayer;
Where duty calls, or danger,
Be never wanting there.

4 Stand up, stand up for Jesus,
The strife will not be long;
This day the noise of battle,
The next the victor's song:
To him that overcometh,
A crown of life shall be;
He with the King of glory
Shall reign eternally.

227. When, His Salvation Bringing.

1 When, his salvation bringing,
To Zion Jesus came,
The children all stood singing
Hosannas to his name.
Nor did their zeal offend him,
For as he rode along,
He let them still attend him,
And smiled to hear their song.

2 And since the Lord retaineth
His love for children still;
Though now as King he reigneth
On Zion's heavenly hill,
We'll flock around his banner,
Who sits upon the throne;
And cry aloud "Hosanna
To David's royal Son!"

3 For should we fail proclaiming
Our great Redeemer's praise:
The stones, our silence shaming
Might well hosannas raise.
But shall we only render
The tribute of our words?
No! while our hearts are tender,
They, too, shall be the Lord's.

228   While Life Prolongs.

1 While life prolongs its precious light
   Mercy is found, and peace is given,
But soon, ah! soon, approaching night
   Shall blot out every hope of heaven.

2 While God invites, how blest the day,
   How sweet the Gospel's charming sound;
Come, sinners, haste, oh, haste away,
   While yet a pardoning God is found.

3 Soon, borne on time's most rapid wing,
   Shall death command you to the grave:
Before his bar your spirits bring,
   And none be found to hear or save.

4 In that lone land of deep despair,
   No Sabbath's heavenly light shall rise—
No God regard your bitter prayer,
   No Saviour call you to the skies.

229   Just as I am.

1 Just as I am, without one plea,
But that thy blood was shed for me,
And that thou bids't me come to thee,
   O Lamb of God, I come! I come!

2 Just as I am, and waiting not
To rid my soul of one dark blot, [spot,
To thee, whose blood can cleanse each
   O Lamb of God, I come! I come!

3 Just as I am, though tossed about
With many a conflict, many a doubt,
Fightings within and fears without,
   O Lamb of God, I come! I come!

4 Just as I am—poor, wretched, blind;
Sight, riches, healing of the mind,
Yea, all I need, in thee to find,
   O Lamb of God, I come! I come!

5 Just as I am—thou wilt receive,
Wilt welcome, pardon, cleanse, relieve,
Because thy promise I believe,
   O Lamb of God, I come! I come!

6 Just as I am—thy love unknown
Hath broken every barrier down;
Now, to be thine, yea, thine alone,
   O Lamb of God, I come! I come!

230   Come, Holy Spirit.

1 Come, Holy Spirit, calm my mind,
   And fit me to approach my God;
Remove each vain, each worldly thought,
   And lead me to thy blest abode.

2 Hast thou imparted to my soul
   A living spark of holy fire?
Oh! kindle now the sacred flame,
   Make me to burn with pure desire.

3 A brighter faith and hope impart,
   And let me now my Saviour see;
Oh! soothe and cheer my burdened heart,
   And bid my spirit rest in thee.

231   When I Survey.

1 When I survey the wondrous cross,
   On which the Prince of Glory died,
My richest gain I count but loss,
   And pour contempt on all my pride.

2 Forbid it, Lord, that I should boast,
   Save in the death of Christ, my God;
All the vain things that charm me most,
   I sacrifice them to his blood.

3 See, from his head, his hands, his feet,
   Sorrow and love flow mingled down;
Did e'er such love and sorrow meet,
   Or thorns compose so rich a crown?

4 His dying crimson, like a robe,
   Spreads o'er his body on the tree,
Then am I dead to all the globe,
   And all the globe is dead to me.

5 Were the whole realm of nature mine,
   That were a present far too small;
Love so amazing, so divine,
   Demands my soul, my life, my all.

TOPICAL INDEX.

ANNIVERSARY, 66, 68, 142, 148, 170, 196.
ASPIRATION, 10, 33.
ASSURANCE, 31, 38, 62, 91.
AWAKENING, 6, 97.
BIBLE, 87.
CHILDREN'S DAY, 129, 146, 147, 186.
CHRISTIAN ACTIVITY, 34, 92, 96.
CHRISTIAN LIVING, 44, 48, 78, 86, 97, 135, 138.
CHRISTIAN WARFARE, 6, 36, 38, 121, 192, 209.
CHRISTMAS, 180, 182, 183, 185.
CLOSING, 85, 120, 127, 219.
COMFORTER, 109.
CONFIDENCE, 31, 38, 55, 94, 102.
CONSOLATION, 81, 82, 136.
EASTER, 32, 79. 174, 188.
ENCOURAGEMENT, 7, 12, 37, 40, 78, 83, 99, 112, 128, 153, 171.
EXPERIENCE, 90, 91, 152.
FAITH, 37, 94, 112.
FELLOWSHIP, 39, 62, 98, 127.
GRACE, 49.
GUIDANCE, 8, 22, 24, 55, 60, 93, 94, 95, 102, 134, 143.
HEAVEN, 9, 27, 28, 50, 64, 73, 74, 168.

HOLY SPIRIT, 109, 114, 165, 230.
INVITATION, 28, 30, 41, 52, 56, 57, 69, 103, 108, 139, 141, 201.
JESUS, 41, 42, 53, 58, 59, 72, 75, 99, 154, 157, 161.
JOY, 104, 123, 124, 142.
JOURNEY, 22, 108, 162.
LOVE, 59, 149, 151, 161, 163.
LOYALTY, 18, 226.
MARCHING, 6, 16, 23, 38, 198.
MISSIONARY, 54, 140, 166, 217.
PEACE, 115.
PRAISE, 25, 66, 68, 76, 116, 124, 130, 142, 145, 148, 158, 196.
PRAYER, 224.
PRIMARY, 40, 47, 71, 104, 105, 172, 173, 175, 177, 178, 179, 188, 199, 206, 208.
PROMISES, 14, 61.
PROVIDENCE, 20, 65, 214.
REDEMPTION, 70, 144.
REPENTANCE, 119, 200, 213, 229.
REST, 162, 195.
SALVATION, 63, 70, 160, 227.
SURETY, 31, 133.
TEMPERANCE, 52, 132, 191, 192.
TRUST, 15, 35, 102.
WORK, 96, 100, 110, 122.

Bright Melodies.

Abide with me..... 127	Fill me now...... 165	I've heard the news. 160
A feast of love to- 151	Fill to overflow- 114	I will say yes to. 200
A golden promise I. 61	Forth in the dawn-. 110	I would be a sunbea 177
A hand all bruised.. 41	Give me Jesus..... 58	Jesus at the helm 154
A light behind... 37	Gladly the bells are. 129	Jesus gives his peace 115
A light in our... 21	Gloria Patri..... 5	Jesus has opened up. 207
A little while to.... 80	Gloria Patri..... 117	Jesus is my joy and 123
All hail the power.. 221	Glorious victory. 36	Jesus is come..... 75
All the fields are gr 166	Glory be to the Fath 5	Jesus is the light... 90
All the way...... 60	God bless the hearts 232	Jesus leads....... 8
A message sweet is. 49	God will remem-.. 179	Jesus leads the w 22
Are you sowing, dail 17	Go forth at Christ's 18	Jesus' little sol- 172
Are you sowing fo 17	Go work to-day... 110	Jesus lives....... 72
Army of the living.. 118		Jesus, lover of my.. 159
As a Christian band 122	Hallelujah! halleluja 70	Jesus promised me 14
A sinner saved... 70	Hallowed be Thy na 194	Jesus, Saviour, pilot 95
As now we part.. 232	Happy children..... 173	Jesus, the beautiful. 107
Awake the songs of. 146	Happy day........ 217	Jesus, the name.... 220
	Hark, hark the trum 6	Journey in the K 108
Banner of the blesse 43	Hear the Master 166	Joy and sunshine. 123
Beautiful carols of j 174	Hear the Saviour sa 19	Joyful praises.... 142
Behold a royal army 16	Hear the words of J 157	Joy to the world.... 223
Be of good cheer... 7	He feedeth His flock 65	Just as I am....... 229
Blessed Bible...... 87	He is mine, I am.. 62	Just one touch..... 139
Blessed Lily of the. 62	He leadeth me..... 55	
Blessed union...... 202	He leadeth safel 102	Keep in heart, be.. 37
Blessed words that. 13	Here in Thy name.. 214	Keep on the sunny 128
Bought on Calvar 144	Holy, holy, holy... 209	
Bright little sun 206	Holy Spirit from ab 109	Lead me, Saviour. 93
By and by I know.. 9	Holy Spirit, Hea 109	Leaning on the ev 98
By grace alone... 49	Hover o'er me, Holy 165	Lend a hand...... ,192
	How blest are we in 140	Let all the earth.... 124
Cheerily on, O Ende 100	How firm a founda- 215	Let me help some 135
Christ is King.... 25	How many sad part- 85	Let us do what we. 71
Come and join our.. 121	How sweet the nam 219	Like a Shepherd, te 8
Come away, the bell 185	How the hand of lov 149	List to the story.... 156
Come, come to-day 141	Hum, little bee, in.. 179	Little bells of Easter 188
Come, every soul by 35		Little trusting... 178
Come, Holy Spirit, c 230	I am coming to the. 216	Living water..... 13
Come into the fol 30	I am thinking to-day 27	Look up, brother... 190
Come, O come..... 207	I am walking in the 51	Lost after all... 69
Come to me....... 201	If clouds blot out... 189	Lord, I care not for. 211
Come to the feast 57	If o'er thy way dark 112	Love Divine....... 163
Come to the Saviour 141	I glory in the cro 32	Love lightens bur 149
Count your bless- 20	In accents of love.. 30	Loyalty to Christ 18
Crossing one by.. 50	In a world where sor 40	
Crossing the bar. 89	In God's own time 112	Make the moments. 138
Crown Him Lord... 221	In that city...... 73	Many souls are sink- 192
	In that fair city.... 64	March, march along 23
Day's bright beams. 176	In the sunshine... 51	March on, happy sol 38
Do not draw the... 153	I read that whoso- 63	Mighty army of the. 72
Don't you know... 81	I shall be satis- 234	More about Jesus.. 33
Do the best you.. 189	I shall lay the cross. 195	More than con-.. 43
Doxology........ 5	I sing the love of J 59	My country, 'tis of.. 101
Draw me still closer. 39	Is my name writte 211	My Father is rich in 105
	I trust Thee, blessed 15	My heart to-day wit 32
Every one is sowing. 67	It was so little..... 26	My Jesus, as Thou. 208
Faithful workers... 96	I've been a wand'rer 200	My Saviour first. 155
Far from the fold... 97		

INDEX

Nature's glad voi	174
Nearer my God to	193
Neither do I con-	119
No danger can my	91
No home! no home!	111
No, not one	99
No scenes of mirth	84
Not a cloud to hide	136
Not always in green	102
No tears in yonder	45
O'er death's sea, in	73
O'er the earth	147
O'er the trackless	150
O for a thousand	222
O happy day that	217
Oh, don't you hear	41
Oh, remember, Jesus	161
Oh, the wondrous	184
Oh, to have the mind	213
Oh, the world has	78
Oh, we love the dais	178
Oh, won't you meet	56
O listen again to the	44
Once more we gath	47
On for Jesus	92
Only trust Him	35
On the battlefield of	34
On the victory s	152
On thy journey to	134
On to glory	198
On to victory	6
Onward Christian s	212
O praise the Lord	158
O Saviour, meet	203
Our barks may be	24
Our Father which	224
Our souls cry out	152
Our strength and	38
Our waiting eyes	88
Out on sin's ocean	132
Over the sea	19
O what everlasting	114
O wonderful river	233
Penitent, sin-confess-	119
Praise God from w	5
Praise Him	196
Praise, joyful praise	142
Praise the Lord, ye	148
Praise the name of	68
Praise to Thee	66
Praise ye Jehovah	130
Precious gifts of	184
Press onward	167
Rejoice in the L	124
Rejoice, rejoice, the	180
Remember, Jesus l	161
Resting by the w	162
Rise and follow	176
Rock of Ages	210
Roll back the s	153
Roses everywhere	186
Roses, roses, sum-	186
Saviour, lead me	93
Scattering precious	86
Scatter sunshine	40
See! they are	132
Send a cheer a	83
Send out the sun-	48
Shining every-	175
Showers of bless-	214
Since Christ thy	91
Singing as we go	170
Sing on	76
Sing, O ye people	145
Sing unto God	116
Softly and tend-	103
Somebody needs just	135
Some glad day	195
Some sweet day	205
Something more of J	10
Sowing good seed	204
Sowing the seed	44
Sow kind deeds	171
Standing on the	118
Stand up, stand up	226
Step by step	199
Sunset and evening	89
Sunshine as you	78
Sunshine in the s	104
Sweeping down the	25
Sweet Sabbath b	187
Sweet the music of	187
Take the world, but	58
Take the world for	54
Tell me the story of	53
That means me	63
The army of the L	121
The beautiful, b	82
The beautiful la	168
The beautiful lig	90
The beautiful s	107
The bells are c	185
The child of a k	105
The coming of the	180
The earth was filled	79
The firm founda-	215
The glad home g	9
The harbor home	52
The harbor lights	150
The home where c	113
The joyful song	16
The Lord is my s	143
The Lord is our R	133
The Lord knoweth	94
The Lord's prayer	224
The Master's work	122
The mind of Jesus	213
The morning light	225
The mountain-path	94
The new song	104
The night has passed	183
The pillar of c	134
There are songs of j	104
There is a beautiful	144
There is joy at C	182
There's a dark and	128
There's a land be-	74
There's a place in h	14
There's a veil that h	60
There's not a friend	99
There's sunshine in	104
The Saviour's little	175
The sweet new n	61
The river of life	235
The words of J	157
They are pushing	83
Thinking of home	64
This life will soon be	56
'Tis sad to think	69
Toilers in the har-	12
Trusting Thee e	15
Unto the haven	24
Upon the rock	31
Victory, victory, glor	36
Waft, ye winds	140
Wait and murmur	113
Waiting on before	12
Wait on the Lord	29
Wake, list'ning	75
We are Jesus' little	206
We are looking	167
We are marching	172
Wear your white rib-	191
Weary soul, by care	201
We come again	46
We have heard of a	168
We'll all meet	85
We're marching on	22
We're marching to a	170
We're sailing in sal-	154
We shall cross the m	50
We shall cross the r	205
We shall stand be-	11
We will keep our	34
What a fellowship	98
What a joyous time	120
What will you do	106
When all thy mer-	218
When Christ a	79
When Christ is in	84
When from the	42
When his salvation	227
When I shall wake	234
When I survey	231
When my life-work	155
When my soul is op-	82
When our ships	126
When our ships have	126
When the mists	137
When the wintry	182
When upon life's bil-	20
When we reach	136
When your spirit	81
Where'er He leads	199
Wheresoe'er we be	21
Where the roses	74
While life prolongs	228
While upon the pil-	162
Will there be any	27
Will you be one	28
Will you come to	57
Within Thy courts	203
With Jesus	42
Wonderful peace	115
Work in the light	100
Would you go rejoic-	108
You're sailing t'ward	52

224

www.ingramcontent.com/pod-product-compliance
Lightning Source LLC
Chambersburg PA
CBHW021841230426
43669CB00008B/1041